BREAKING SHIPS

How Supertankers and Cargo Ships
Are Dismantled on the Beaches of Bangladesh

Roland Buerk

with photographs by the author

Foreword by Michael Sanders

Chamberlain Bros.
a member of Penguin Group (USA) Inc.
New York

CHAMBERLAIN BROS.
Published by the Penguin Group
Penguin Group (USA) Inc., 375 Hudson Street, New York, New York 10014,
USA • Penguin Group (Canada), 90 Eglinton Avenue East, Suite 700,
Toronto, Ontario M4P 2Y3, Canada (a division of Pearson Penguin
Canada Inc.) • Penguin Books Ltd, 80 Strand, London WC2R 0RL, England
• Penguin Ireland, 25 St Stephen's Green, Dublin 2, Ireland (a division of
Penguin Books Ltd) • Penguin Group (Australia), 250 Camberwell Road,
Camberwell, Victoria 3124, Australia (a division of Pearson Australia Group
Pty Ltd) • Penguin Books India Pvt Ltd, 11 Community Centre, Panchsheel
Park, New Delhi–110 017, India • Penguin Group (NZ), Cnr Airborne and
Rosedale Roads, Albany, Auckland 1310, New Zealand (a division of
Pearson New Zealand Ltd) • Penguin Books (South Africa) (Pty) Ltd,
24 Sturdee Avenue, Rosebank, Johannesburg 2196, South Africa

Penguin Books Ltd, Registered Offices:
80 Strand, London WC2R 0RL, England

Library of Congress Cataloging-in-Publication Data

Buerk, Roland.
Breaking ships : how supertankers and cargo ships are dismantled
on the beaches of Bangladesh / [Roland Buerk].
p.   cm.
Includes index.
ISBN 1-59609-036-7
1. Ships—Scrapping—Bangladesh—Chittagong.   I. Title.
VM149.B76   2005   2005049652
623.82'4—dc22

Printed in the United States of America
1   3   5   7   9   10   8   6   4   2

Book design by Elke Sigal

For Anna

CONTENTS

T here are few sights more humbling than a man bearing a terrible load on his shoulders, working in mud and filth for a pittance, who can still raise a smile. That was the scene that greeted me every day on the beach at Chittagong, in Bangladesh. There, tens of thousands of men labor night and day to turn the world's discarded ships into scrap. The work is hard. Some venture deep into the darkened, oil-stained holds of tankers with blowtorches to cut up the vessels. Their jobs in the tropical heat are not only physically tough but dangerous as well. Men have lost their lives in sudden devastating explosions. Others haul the metal up the beach, lifting great weights with skinny arms, or stagger on thin legs out onto the mudflats, carrying steel ropes and heavy pipes. In the rainy season it is worse. Then the ground underfoot turns into a quagmire. It is a remarkable display of the strength of the human spirit that men can not just endure such conditions but also find some joy amid their hardship.

This book follows the entire process of breaking up the *Asian Tiger*, an enormous oil tanker that weighed thirty-eight thousand tons. She was rammed onto the beach one fine day in spring 2004. That morning we met the ship's new owner, Mohammed

Mohsin, at a pontoon on the Karnaphuli River. It was just up-stream from where the mouth of the river meets the Bay of Bengal, and the perfect place to board our boat out of sight of the pier masters keen to collect a toll. We puttered across the water in a small hand-built wooden boat toward the motor launch that would take us out to the tanker. The harsh sunlight bounced off the water and, despite the early hour, everyone sweated gently in the humid heat.

Getting on board the *Asian Tiger* was no easy task. She towered over our small launch as we drew up to her side. There was a precarious scramble up a wooden rope ladder before we reached her long, steep gangplank. Once we were on the deck it seemed impossible to us that men could even conceive of trying to break her up—she looked as invulnerable as a city block, and as massive. The ship appeared to be in good condition, too. There was little rust and her paintwork was still bright. Everything seemed to be in fully working order. It was only economics that had condemned her to end her days in Chittagong, no longer a viable working vessel because insuring her and her cargoes had become too expensive.

On the last miles of her lifetime's journey, the *Asian Tiger* surged through the waters of the Bay of Bengal, moving as powerfully as she had on her ocean crossings carrying crude from the Middle East to the tiger economies of Southeast Asia. This was not a ship staggering and gasping to the scrapper's yard, at risk of sinking at any moment. Her propeller was still thudding the sea, churning the water into a long wake, when she hit the shore.

It was only at that moment that she suddenly stopped being a vessel and became a lump of scrap. She was so vast that at sea the movement of her hull with the waves had been almost imperceptible, but once the movement stopped as her hull hit bottom and she was no longer floating, the difference was immediately obvious. Everyone felt it, as the life went out of her. Tears pricked the eyes of the tough seamen who had worked on board the vessel. At that moment the *Asian Tiger* died. She was not a ship anymore, but a giant piece of steel now abandoned on the beach—the detritus of the industrialized world left to be disposed of by the poor.

The shipping industry relies on the willingness of nations like Bangladesh to handle its garbage—dangerous, dirty, and polluting as it is. The ship-breaking beaches of Chittagong, in Bangladesh, Alang, in India, and other places in benighted parts of the world may seem a long way from the soaring cities of the West, but they are a part of the process, too. Almost every product imaginable is transported by sea; the work on the beach is a vital part of the finances of the shipping industry, a fiercely competitive world. It has been estimated that breaking a ship on the coast of America would cost at least $14 million. Now the vessels are sent to the Third World at the end of their useful lives, and shipping lines are able to sell them for cash. Old, outdated vessels that in previous years were viewed only as a liability are now an asset. It helps to keep down the shipping industry's costs as well as, ultimately, the price of goods. Everything would cost us more if poor men were not willing to do this work for so little reward.

As the great ship's journey ended at Chittagong, mine began.

Again and again I drove along the coast road, turning off down the narrow lane paved with blackened cinders to the beach and the ship-breaking yard to see how progress was coming along. At first, not much seemed to happen. Although tiny streamers of orange sparks drifted along the hull as men worked with their blowtorches inside, they seemed to be making little impression on the ship. But then as the days turned into weeks, large chunks began to be cut away. The sweeping lines of the *Asian Tiger* were torn apart into jagged edges. Once the operation was fully under way, the process of destruction was remarkably efficient and quick. It takes far less time to destroy than to build, and she was reduced to the raw materials from which she was made in a matter of months.

Every day I ate in the cheap restaurants where the workers took their meager meals—breakfast and lunch—at a few cents a time. They welcomed me into their homes, huts made of mud and straw where they rested after exhausting shifts at work, and into their lives. They told me about their hopes and dreams and their disappointments. Like everyone, all they were looking for and striving after was a better life for themselves and their children.

I traveled to the north of Bangladesh, a beautiful place that seemed to an outsider like some kind of rural idyll, where people still live by tilling the land according to ancient methods, and carts drawn by oxen make their way home from the fields at sunset along the pathways shaded by banana trees. And I heard men there tell of the lives of excruciating poverty they led. It was all very well, the vivid greens of the countryside and the clean air, but there were few work opportunities and little to eat. Grinding hopelessness made them think that anything was better, even a risky job on the beach, carrying steel for a dollar a day.

I also saw another side of the industry—those who had become rich buying ships and selling the scrap steel. I visited them in their comfortable mansions in the best parts of the city and ate with them in the finest restaurants. They were equally welcoming, the wealthy and the poor. It is easy to condemn from the comfort of an armchair in a prosperous Western nation those who run such industries that pollute and exploit. But those I met, at least, were decent men with true convictions. They were open, and willing to let me see a business they are convinced operates not only for their personal profit but also because their country, in order to develop, needs the steel they provide.

They genuinely believed they were doing their best for Bangladesh in circumstances that were far from ideal. They kept telling me it was a dirty job but someone had to do it.

So this is the story of all their lives over six months in 2004, the year they killed the *Asian Tiger*.

—Roland Buerk, Dhaka, May 2005

I n recent times, one recurrent vogue among contemporary historians, journalists, and other nonfiction writers has been to jump headlong into one *really large subject,* to untangle its processes and introduce its personalities, and then subsequently to try to make some sense of it all for the reader. Often, such topics look back to the past, rekindling the excitement of an almost forgotten triumph or adventure, or more purely ring the bells of nostalgia and that longing for a simpler time which seems such a common thread these days. Salt, chocolate, longitude, steel, a warship, the plague, a racehorse—these are just a few recent examples, to which we could add all of those books whose subtitles contain the phrase "And How It Changed the World" or "The Making Of. . .".

Partly, I think, this phenomenon betrays the anxiety of a culture living in an era of breathtaking, and breathtakingly paced, change, when we look to the past for reassurance, when the icons of our history, recent or not so, take on the enhanced power to remind us of our own strengths at a time when the future can seem so uncertain. Partly, too, it reflects the influence of popular culture, when it is no longer sufficient to watch a movie and be enthralled by the acting, the sets, and the story. Today, we have to know how such and such a shot was set up, why the cameraman chose this filter for that scene, and that the gaffer's thoughts during filming were with his mum, battling a life-threatening disease.

Being a contrarian reader, I find nostalgia cloying in more than a minuscule dose, and a welter of irrelevant detail and background equally tiresome. The "Making of" narrative template, too, can sometimes feel like one too many pieces of pie at the picnic. How rare it is, then, to come across Roland Buerk's *Breaking Ships*, a book which is none of those things, but rather an unexpected and refreshing work about the *unmaking* of a very large thing—the *Asian Tiger*, a thirty-eight-thousand-ton oil tanker, and its dismantling steel plate by steel plate on a beach in Bangladesh.

Buerk's very stark narrative, leanly related, resonated very personally with me from start to finish: while I wrote about the construction of a ship by hand from stem to fantail, he tells the tale in reverse, its destruction from radar mast to keel, also virtually by hand. Just as there is a logic to a ship's building, its unbuilding proceeds according to certain accepted notions, too, and few of them obvious! Today, many ships are built in modular pieces first, the pieces then bolted and welded together at the seams. Their breaking is also done in sections, and the cutter's goal is quite simply efficiency—that the pieces land flat (hull) side down, giving the beach crews on the ground easy access for their own torches on the way to cut the steel down to manageable pieces.

Where I related the thrill of launch, *Breaking Ships* begins with an act that goes against the grain of every ship captain: running his ship at full steam right onto the beach at high tide, as fast and far as he can go. Just about there, I realized that even my modest knowledge of shipbuilding was not going to be of much use on this journey, so different is that world from a modern shipyard. In Chittagong, Bangladesh, you can tell the cutters on deck not by their hard hats but because they are actually wearing shoes and coveralls, unlike the gangs of laborers below, who spend their days, dawn to dusk, hauling half-ton plates of steel on their shoulders through the mud and muck, searing heat and monsoon rain, from ship to shore. Barefoot.

From that first shock of an intentional beaching, Buerk's exploration of Chittagong opens out to embrace a brutal and unforgiving world that has more than a few lessons and insights for the rest of us, for this is not a simple tale of men and cutting torches. Thirty-year-old Mohammed Mohsin pays $15 million for the salvage rights to the *Asian Tiger*; that shoeless steel hauler earns a few dollars a day. How easy it is to condemn the Cartier watch and Hermès suit of the one and to bemoan the injustice of the wages of the other. And yet Mohsin provides a living, directly and indirectly, for thousands and thousands of young men who would otherwise live in even more abject poverty in their inland villages.

On a trip back to one isolated village with a recruiter, Buerk humanizes this alien world, brings it into sharper focus. Many of these young men have families, from whom they must live apart for months on end while working at a dangerous, unhealthy, and potentially life-threatening job. Yet when we meet them, meet their wives and children, that choice to go to Chittagong seems more comprehensible, a chance however tentative to better their lives, support their extended families, send their children to school.

The ship-breaking industry up and down the beaches of Chittagong has spawned scores of recycling, refurbishing, and re-sale businesses that offer everything from fire extinguishers to life boats (favored by the local fishermen), navigation equipment to chunks of polystyrene foam, all of which would otherwise simply be dumped. The only thing that defeats the breakers is the engine itself, at the size of a modest house just too large and unwieldy to salvage in one piece for reuse.

The steel from the ships gave rise to a whole industry that today supplies the entire domestic needs of the country for certain kinds of structural steel used in the building trades, steel which would otherwise have to be imported at great cost to one of the poorest nations in the world. In one of the more fascinating chapters, we watch as the steel plate cut one day from the ship is reforged and reshaped—that night—into reinforcing rod bound for a building site the day after. In perhaps the ultimate contradiction, Buerk points out that the ship breakers sometimes don't even make a profit on the steel. The sheer volume of recycled steel and ship fittings is one of the only sources of cash money, capital, available in a Muslim country (where usury is more than frowned upon) and access to government loans involves running a gauntlet of corrupt bureaucrats, each one with his hand out.

Environmentally, of course, there is a high cost to pay. Although ship breaking started in this region with the accidental grounding of a single ship some years ago, today it is an industry, and a very dirty one, with few if any environmental controls. Aside from the spilled oil, ship breaking has contaminated the land with heavy metals like cadmium and mercury, and other toxic materials like asbestos abound, too. It is also such an environmentally destructive industry that it can exist only in a few places—Bangladesh, Pakistan, China—because the rest of the world, and certainly the developed world, won't have it. (So be careful where you point your finger when you're looking for someone to blame.)

In what is perhaps the heaviest irony of all, ship breaking in Bangladesh may be coming to an end, this industry, like garment making before it, flowing to China. And it is not that Chinese workers will work for less money, either, but that the furnaces of their steel mills have an insatiable hunger for steel to recycle. The mill has to be close to its source in order for the endeavor to make any economic sense. The Mohsin family conglomerate and a group of other ship breakers are currently looking for a billion dollars to build a steel mill. After reading *Breaking Ships*, it's hard not to hope they find it.

—Michael Sanders, author of *The Yard*,
Families of the Vine,
and *From Here, You Can't See Paris*

The bow of the Asian Tiger

CHAPTER ONE

LAST VOYAGE

"There she is," says Captain Enam Mohammed Chowdhury, pointing at a ship looming out of the early morning haze that hangs over the greasy rolling waters of the Bay of Bengal. "That's the one." Even from more than a mile away, the tanker looks huge. She dwarfs the container ships moored around her in the outer anchorage off the port of Chittagong, in Bangladesh. The wooden coasters with high bows and sterns, built in a style unchanged over the centuries, look like specks as they inch past her, carrying their cargoes of rice and straw.

Beside Captain Enam in the wheelhouse of the motor launch *Sea Petrel*, Mohammed Mohsin smiles. This is his first glimpse of his new ship. The thirty-year-old had bought her over the telephone for $15 million without seeing even a photograph. All that mattered was the weight of the steel that made up her structure, and the price. But he is pleased with what he sees. "She's cute," he says with a broad grin on his face.

Captain Enam stares intently as the launch draws nearer. He strokes his long beard—dyed orange with henna to conceal the gray of middle age. He grabs a large pair of old binoculars from a shelf above the wheel and scrambles out onto the small deck at the back of the boat for a closer look. "Go around her," he shouts to the helmsman. "I need to check her trim."

Emptied of her last cargo of oil, she rides high in the water. Her shiny bronze propeller is only half submerged. The blades standing out of the water are massively thick and longer than four men are tall. Her rudder is like the wing of an airliner, and the side of her hull is a cliff rearing straight up from the sea. The paint to protect her from corrosion is a dark dull red. Toward the waterline, she's dotted with living barnacles and old chalky shells. It takes a long time for the launch to travel her length, the motor puttering and spluttering as she noses slowly through the water. Captain Enam nods with quiet satisfaction as the boat bobs under the jutting bow and into the cool shadow cast by the ship. The crew has carried out his orders to shift as much of the ballast as possible toward the stern. That way she'll ride light at the bow and come to a halt farther up the beach when he runs her aground. High above his head, the ship's name is written in square white letters ten feet tall: *ASIAN TIGER*.

Captain Enam kills ships for a living. For fourteen years he has been steering them onto the flat muddy beaches north of Chittagong. He long ago lost count of the number he's dispatched in this way, but it is definitely more than nine hundred, perhaps even as many as a thousand. The months of late spring, when the high tides are at their peak, are his busiest of the year. All sorts of ships have passed through his hands over the years, large and small. The previous day he piloted an old container ship on its final journey; tomorrow it might be a passenger liner; today it is the turn of the *Asian Tiger*, an oil tanker. Being the executioner of ships is a highly specialized business, and Captain Enam is known as the best in Bangladesh. Seamen spend their working lives trying to avoid the shore, anxious to prevent their vessels from running aground—doing the opposite does not come naturally to most.

The Asian Tiger *with a piece already cut from her side*

Climbing up the side of the Asian Tiger

Captain Enam chose his unusual job after years at sea. He had sailed all over the world and enjoyed it, but the voyages had kept him away from home for months on end. As he had gotten older, he had decided he wanted a job that allowed him to go home to his wife every night. Becoming a killer of ships had been the perfect option.

The *Sea Petrel* draws up to the rope ladder that had been lowered down the ship's side. Captain Enam hitches up his khaki trousers, shoulders his small rucksack, and puts his baseball cap on backward to climb up to the deck far above. The tiny motor launch bobs and bumps against the tanker. The *Asian Tiger* is so large she's impervious to the motion of the waves in all but the fiercest storm. Here in the calm waters of an early morning it is as if she is rooted to the seabed, she is so steady.

Captain Enam looks up at the hull; it is a long way to the top. First he scrambles up the ladder, fifteen feet of wooden rungs banging against the hull with each step. Then he hauls himself on to the metal gangway that leads the rest of the way. It is steep because it had been designed to be used when the ship was laden and far lower in the water. Even though the sun is just up over the horizon, it is hot and humid. But used to clambering about on ships, Captain Enam does not break into a sweat. A crewman in a white boiler suit is waiting for him as he reaches the top and looks around.

"Beaching captain, welcome aboard," he says.

"A very good morning," replies Captain Enam. "Haul up the anchors, leave them two meters from the water for emergency braking, port and starboard sides."

"Yes, sir," says the crewman and heads toward the bow.

Captain Enam turns in the opposite direction and walks toward the white superstructure at the tanker's stern, across the expanse of the deck that is interrupted only by great pipes that run the length of the vessel and into the holds. He steps into the cool of the apartment-block-size complex of cabins and offices, so large it has its own elevator to carry the crew between the floors, from their cabins to the engine room and the office and the other places of work. Captain Enam presses the button for the bridge. The Chinese captain of the *Asian Tiger,* Hou De Qi, meets him there. "Beaching captain, you have command."

In that moment, the *Asian Tiger* is formally handed over from the man whose job had been to protect her from harm to her executioner.

A clanking begins to reverberate through the ship. The anchors are dragged from the seabed by the mighty winches in the bow, and she is getting under way. Link after link of the massive chains comes out of the ocean, cascading water and mud. The chains are still dripping as they're heaved up over the side and into the lockers. The winch engines roar and the chains rumble over the gearwheels. Slowly the ship builds up speed. After twenty-eight years and millions of sea miles, the *Asian Tiger* is beginning her final journey.

On the bridge, First Officer Simon Aung leans on the chart table, where the map "Approaches to Chittagong" is spread out, to fill in the engine movement log. "This will be the last page," he says somberly to the rest of the crew.

Captain Enam clears his throat and issues the order "Full steam ahead." The rumble from the engines far below moves up a pitch. The crew stands at their stations around the bridge, looking over the controls in their pale blue painted panels, watching the flickering lights, and pressing the buttons and switches necessary to control the vessel. One mans the radio, another's at the helm. The wheel they use to steer so big an oil tanker is surprisingly small. The bridge is a utilitarian room in which to spend so many months, made of hard metal surfaces with few concessions to comfort. But the men have attempted to make it more homey.

Captain Enam boards the ship

A last look at the charts

In one corner, a creeping plant grows out of a pot, spreading its green tendrils across the ceiling.

The principle of beaching a ship is simple. The vessel is sailed a few miles out to sea, turned toward the land, and, at as high a speed as possible, driven onto the shore. The closer she ends up to the high-water mark, the easier and cheaper she will be to scrap. The previous day, at low tide, workers from the ship-breaking yard had struggled out onto the mudflats with long bamboo poles and red flags. They had planted them in three pairs extending out to sea. They were laid out like a series of soccer goalposts a hundred meters wide. The first set was a hundred meters off shore, the second a hundred meters beyond that, the third three hundred meters out. It is a small and precise target, barely wider than the ship is broad.

The skill of the beaching captain is in judging the effects of the tide and the wind as he brings the vessel in. The *Asian Tiger* will be pushed off course all the way. She can't simply be aimed straight at the shore but must come in at angle, slipping to one side or the other as the forces of nature work on her.

"Once, another beaching captain was drunk," says Mohammed Mohsin. "He put a ship into the yard next door. It couldn't be brought off, so the owners had to come to a deal."

Hou De Qi, now the captain of the *Asian Tiger* in name only, stands in his cabin one floor down, staring out the window. From there he can see the length of the vessel, across the deck extending more than a hundred meters and lined with pipes and catwalks, and rising up slightly in the distance to the bow.

The captain's cabin on the *Asian Tiger* is like a small hotel suite. There's a lounge area with thick carpet and sofas gathered around a coffee table. There is a desk to work at and cupboards for the captain's possessions, though Hou De Qi doesn't have many. On the wall are gauges for monitoring the movement of the ship. A small bedroom leads off the living area.

Captain Hou De Qi's holdall is already packed with everything he wants to salvage from his life onboard the *Asian Tiger*. It's waiting by the door, ready to go. This is the end of his relationship with this ship. He will get another, but there's a bond between a captain and his command.

"Last night all the guys had a party," he says, blinking hard. "Some of the young guys cried. After the party I came to my cabin. I thought I wouldn't cry, but I did cry a bit."

Up on the bridge, Captain Enam is peering at the distant shoreline through binoculars.

"There are the flags," he says. "Steering zero six five."

"Zero six five," comes the reply from the helmsman.

The *Asian Tiger* begins a long turn, so slow and so ponderous it feels as if the ship is standing still and the world is moving around her. Slowly, the horizon swivels and the ship heads toward the distant shore, the low, pointed hills behind the beach gray in the distance. Thet Wo, the ship's pump man from Myanmar, is standing at the back of the bridge looking mournful, his boiler suit and hard hat blackened with oil.

"Am I sad?" he asks. "Of course. This ship has been like a home to me."

The bridge is quiet. The crew doesn't speak. For all of them on board, apart from Captain Enam, this is their first experience of a beaching. It is a somber occasion, but exciting too, and they wait for the end.

Captain Enam paces from port to starboard and back again. He stops to look again through his binoculars. Hou De Qi had come back up the bridge to watch the last miles of the *Asian Tiger*'s long, lifetime journey. The two men stand side by side and talk about the finer points of this particular ship's handling.

Then the beaching captain moves over to the radar. He sits at the stool behind the screen. His eyes flicker up and down from the figures and markings on the screen to the way ahead. He cal-

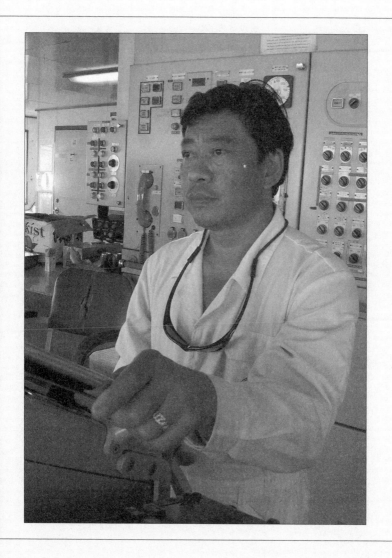

First Officer Aung steers her in

Pump man Wo on the bridge

culates the effect of the wind and the tide by doing sums and by instinct. The ship is being pushed hard toward the north—she's coming in to the beach at the wrong angle. It's only a slight error, but it will be enough to leave her hundreds of meters off course if it's not corrected.

"Steering starboard five," he orders.

"Starboard five," the helmsman replies, as he grips the wheel hard.

Mohammed Mohsin taps his fingers nervously on the sill under the windows at the front of the bridge. Like everyone else on board he's staring ahead intently. He's a businessman, not a seaman. All the risk of the beaching going wrong is his, but he can play no role in the process other than as a spectator.

"Look at all those fishermen ahead," he says, pointing at a flotilla of frail wooden boats in the oil tanker's path. The men on the boats are standing up and gesturing frantically. The ship draws closer rapidly, and it seems as if the nearest boat will be rammed, crushed into the sea. But they all just clear the mighty ship and slip along the side safely as the *Asian Tiger* sweeps past. Soon they are left far astern, bouncing and rocking on the great ship's wake. "They do that deliberately, you know," says Mohammed Mohsin. "Tomorrow they'll bring old torn nets to my office and ask for money. Look at that guy waving for us to move out of the way. Excuse me."

By now there's just one mile left to go. The shore looms close and thickly green under the bow. The palm trees sway in the breeze. It could almost be a tropical holiday paradise but for the dozens of half-dismantled ships already drawn up along the beach stretching away for miles to the north and the south. Individual men on the shore can now be picked out, even though their ragged dirty work clothes blend in with the mud littered with torn metal and rust and oil. They pause in their task of cutting up the remnants of the last vessel to watch the next one come in.

The local children are there to see the show, too. They dance about with excitement as the massive tanker draws nearer.

Half a mile out, and the *Asian Tiger* is still running full speed ahead. She leaves a long wake behind her as her propeller churns the brown water.

"I'm getting more and more tense now," says Mohammed Mohsin. "I hope it's a good beaching."

The crew in the bridge stares forward. The helmsman's face has a look of fixed concentration. Captain Enam's commands come faster now.

"Port five."

"Port five," the instant reply.

"Rudder amidships."

"Rudder amidships."

The ship races forward, surging through the water. The beach with the workers and children disappears from view, hidden by the high bow, far forward from the bridge.

"That's it, we're past the first flags," shouts Mohammed Mohsin. Then, almost imperceptibly, the ship begins to slow down and to touch bottom. She slides along the seabed now, her hull slipping through the smooth mud. Even though she is running aground she still has a lot of way on her. An oil tanker with the momentum of its great weight takes a lot of stopping.

"That's the second set of flags," shouts Mohammed Mohsin. "It's good."

Then, gradually, the ship begins to halt. It takes the crew on board a while to be certain it's happening. There are no sudden judders or shakes, no crashes or groans from the hull, just a slight feeling of slowing down, of being pushed forward where they stand as the ship loses speed. She comes to a rest right between the flags. The flags still stand in the water just a few meters from either side of the hull. The giant vessel has been placed on the beach with almost perfect accuracy. "Turn off the engine. We

Captain Qi and Captain Enam on the bridge

The view from the bridge, half a mile from shore

don't need it anymore," says Captain Enam. From bow to stern, the ship falls silent.

"This is the first time there has been no sound on board," says First Officer Aung. "Even in port we always had at least a generator going."

Captain Enam replies: "She has traveled for so many miles, now she's going for her final rest. Bless her."

The Chinese captain takes a last photograph of the bridge where he had exercised his command. The crewmen shake hands and pick up their bags. All they had saved from the *Asian Tiger,* other than their few personal possessions, were the ship's charts.

Some take one last look around the superstructure that had been their home for months or years: The kitchen lined with steel units and work surfaces, where the walk-in fridge is still full of fruit and Cokes. The cabins scattered with unwanted, abandoned belongings. Posters left on the walls, magazines and books littering the floors and left half read and open on coffee tables. Unmade beds. Office chairs pushed back from the desks as if the men who worked there were about to return. The clocks on the walls ticking. The calendars on the walls open to that day's date.

The living quarters of the ship are now completely deserted.

The crew walks out in small groups into the sunshine of the deck and toward the gangway. They joke and laugh as they scramble into lifeboats salvaged from some other ship for the short journey to the shore, already looking forward to the flight home and months of leave. As they walk up the beach through crowds of curious yard workers, most take one last look back at the ship before climbing into a bus. Then they are gone.

Beached, the *Asian Tiger* is no longer a living vessel but a thirty-eight-thousand-ton lump of imported mild steel. The huge task of cutting her up is about to begin.

A PHP truck

CHAPTER TWO

THE OWNER

T he goat bleats plaintively as it is hoisted up the side of the *Asian Tiger* in a wooden crate suspended on the end of a long rope. All four of its legs are tied together with a piece of dirty string, leaving it pinioned, barely able to move, and certainly beyond making a frantic leap for freedom. The crew of the ship is long gone. She has been handed over to the workers of PHP, the ship-breaking yard owned by Mohammed Mohsin's family. They will destroy her.

On the beach there's always a blood sacrifice before work begins to break up a new vessel. It's a tradition that's keenly watched by all the men on the beach.

The crowd moves forward to watch the goat coming up and over the side, eager to ensure each step of the ritual is carried out in accordance with tradition. As soon as the crate reaches the top, they heave it over the ship's railings and lift the animal out onto the deck. It fights against its bonds, thrashing helplessly before it seems to accept its fate and lies still.

The men recite prayers at the bow of the great oil tanker as they slit the goat's throat with three sawing cuts of a long knife, back and forth. The blade had been sharpened to a razor edge, and the animal's neck is severed almost to the backbone. As the blood pumps out, the men carry the dying goat around, spreading the gore as far as possible. Some is collected in little pots and spattered in the far corners of the ship. It is a big vessel, but they try to get at least a few drops in every section. While the goat's carcass is still warm, it is crudely butchered on the deck and cut into rough chunks. The meat is distributed first among those who will work on board the vessel, the cutters.

The cutters have the most dangerous job in the ship-breaking yard. They have the most to gain if the sacrifice delivers the results for which all the men hope—they also have the most to lose if it does not. They will have to venture deep into the darkened, stranded hulk of the vessel to slice her into pieces with primitive blowtorches. Deaths are not uncommon in the ship-breaking yards of Chittagong, and the ship cutters' place of work means they are the most vulnerable. Gas buildups can cause sudden explosions that sweep through the holds of vessels with devastating effects.

"The workers believe the ship demands blood," says the owner of the PHP breaking yard, Mohammed Mohsin. "She doesn't care if it's the blood of men or of goats, so we let all the blood run, right across the deck."

Mohsin is not a particularly superstitious man, but he too feels better once everything possible has been done to appease fate and whatever malevolence the men believe the ship might feel about her fate. He and his family have borrowed $15 million to buy the *Asian Tiger*. It is a massive roll of the dice, a six-month gamble on the world price of steel that Mohsin will have to oversee to a successful conclusion. Ship-breaking can be a risky business, for worker and owner alike. All his life, says Mohsin, he has been fascinated by the death of the ships in the breaking yard.

"I remember coming to this beach as a boy and collecting discarded nuts and bolts," he reminisces. "My father used to give me ten taka [twenty cents] a kilogram."

It had been an early lesson in the economics of an industry that was raw capitalism, as red in tooth and claw as it got. As an adult Mohsin is doing much the same thing, but on a far bigger scale. He is still collecting metal to sell it by weight. Now it is by the tens of thousands of tons.

The sacrifice over, Mohsin leads the way, clambering back down the gangway, which still stretches diagonally from the deck to a few meters above the waterline. He climbs carefully down the rope ladder and into the old lifeboat for the short journey to the shore. On the beach, standing among his employees, the owner of the yard is easy to pick out: the workers wear plastic sandals and their legs are filthy to the knee, while Mohsin makes his way carefully through the oil and mud, trying not to mess up his fancy polished black leather loafers. They wear filthy frayed shirts and *lungis*, the traditional skirtlike wrap of a Bangladeshi man; Mohsin wears a gold Rolex and his clothes are mostly by Versace. Today he is wearing a pair of black trousers with the logo prominent in the weave, repeated up and down his legs. The men who work in the ship-breaking yard are slight and skinny; they have come to the beach to escape some of the most poverty-stricken regions of a desperately poor country. Mohsin is well fed and glossy, and he is not unaware of his good fortune.

Mohsin always carries two cell phones, which chirp continuously all day. Every few minutes he breaks off from what he's doing for shouted conversations with whoever's at the other end of the crackling line; the suppliers or customers or, more usually, his minions. Often he has one set to each ear simultaneously. Mohsin is just thirty years old, and he's running firms worth millions of dollars. Constant vigilance and attention are needed to keep the businesses ticking and running smoothly.

PHP employs thousands of people. There are the rerolling mills, the zinc galvanizing works, the oxygen factory. As well as overseeing the arrival of the *Asian Tiger* that week, Mohsin is helping one of his six younger brothers, Sohel, organize the building of Bangladesh's first float-glass factory. It will reduce the country's reliance on imports for the perfectly smooth, flat windows produced using the modern technique. Both spend all day on their phones giving the managers on the ground their instructions. It is an enormous project, the hi-tech building covering acres of land on a site a few miles from the ship-breaking yard. Mohsin is plainly in his element, wheeling and dealing, persuading recalcitrant bureaucrats that, yes, they should move that electricity pylon that is in the way. Sohel will take time to become as assured as his older brother. Running the place is his first job now that he's back from attending college in Australia. While his classmates from university in Canberra are starting out at the bottom of the ladder, he's getting a boost straight to the top. The brothers can't complain, but it is a heavy responsibility for young shoulders to bear.

PHP is still very much a family firm, but it has grown rapidly to become one of the biggest conglomerates in Bangladesh. The company was founded by Mohammed Mohsin's father, Mizanur Rahman. The name had been the older man's idea. PHP stands for Peace, Happiness, and Prosperity. It is not just what the family hopes their enterprise will bring for them and their country, it is also an acknowledgment of Mizanur Rahman's deep religious faith. In the Koran that is how Prophet Mohammed is often described—as the way to peace, happiness, and prosperity.

Mizanur Rahman is an extraordinary man. He is a millionaire many times over who claims he has no need of money. He has pursued and achieved great wealth with a single-minded determination all his life, but now in his later years, when he has cash in abundance, he truly seems to believe that all you need is

The owner, Mohsin (right), and his brother look at the charts

love. In his case, it is the love of Allah. He beams as he lectures his visitors.

"What do we need?" the man who has built an empire says. "Food, these few clothes that I'll take off later, nothing more."

Mizanur Rahman is a follower of Sufism, a mystical branch of Islam that stresses the importance of a personal relationship with Allah. He is at peace as only a man of deep faith can be.

Mizanur Rahman looks every inch the patriarch. In accordance with Islamic tradition, he has been growing his beard since the last time he went on the hajj pilgrimage to Mecca, and by now it is long and silver. He always wears the same simple outfit: a knee-length cotton shirt and baggy trousers, sandals on his feet, a skullcap on his head. It's a matter of pride to him that the clothes were bought from the market for a few dollars. They are identical to what almost every other older man in Bangladesh wears, whether he is rich or poor. Every day Mizanur Rahman travels to PHP's suite of offices in the old part of Chittagong to hold court. People wait for him to discuss business or to ask for his advice.

Sitting in the back of one of his fleet of Land Cruiser Prados, Mizanur Rahman gazes out complacently as the chauffeur inches the gleaming vehicle through the narrow streets. They were laid out at a time when rickshaws, which take up rather less room on the roads than SUVs, were the only form of wheeled transport in Bangladesh. The tricycle vehicles are still there in great number, lumbering haphazardly around the corners with their bells tinkling and the passengers bouncing on the narrow benches behind the sweating riders. The tricycle vehicles are boldly decorated with bright designs painted on the hoods and seats—stars of Indian films, mosques, and animals. Their presence forces Mizanur Rahman's driver to be even more particular in his movements if he is not to scratch the boss's car. The streets are regularly blocked when trucks try to make their way through to deliver goods. There are jams of handcarts. Devices made of wooden platforms supported on two car wheels are used to move huge quantities of heavy goods like cement by muscle power alone, the skinny pullers straining to take them up the hills or running to keep up on downward stretches.

Mizanur Rahman and his chauffeur drive past the tiny shops cramming each side of the streets of the old town. Customers have to step over the open drains to get inside. Some merchants are selling rice and chilies out of cloth sacks, the tops rolled down so the goods are on display. They measure out the amounts carefully, holding up old-fashioned brass scales and adding the iron weights one by one until both sides balance. Others stock vegetables and fruit. When there are no buyers around, they occupy themselves by polishing the produce and piling it into precise pyramids to look more alluring. There are shops selling aluminum pots and pans, plastic buckets, dusters made from chicken feathers, wires, and metal stakes. There's a man who specializes in repairing guns. He works at a bench in his tiny premises under the light of a dim bulb. All manner of goods are available here. Commerce has always gone on like this in Chittagong, small merchants locked in fierce competition with each other. Little has changed over the decades, or even the centuries, and by basing himself here, Mizanur Rahman is showing that he's still in touch with where he began, even though he has risen so high.

It also makes financial sense. In Bangladesh, the banking system is still decentralized, and personal contacts count. Only the manager of the local branch of a bank can authorize a loan to a businessman. Mizanur Rahman has spent decades building up a relationship of trust with his financiers in Chittagong's old town. If he moves his headquarters, he will have to start the process again with new bankers.

Mizanur Rahman's office is small for a rich man in a country where even the lowliest village bureaucrat enjoys a room big enough for rows of supplicants to sit all day, sniggering along sycophantically until offered the chance to beg their particular favor. Mizanur Rahman has space for just two chairs, apart from his own. He has a reason for that, and he has passed it on to his son Mohsin, who has an even tinier office next door. The room of the boss, he says, is there for him to think up new business ideas. Allowing too many people in is a distraction. PHP's visitors have to wait their turn in an anteroom to see the chairman and his son. Mizanur Rahman has similar ideas about cell phones.

"It's there for my use," he says. "When I've finished talking I switch it off."

Mizanur Rahman's desk is obviously expensive and custom made, but it's also understated, a plain curve of fine wood. Cupboards and drawers built in along two sides of the room are topped by a work surface at waist height. It's covered with dozens of photographs of Mizanur Rahman and his sons with the great and good of Bangladesh. There is the family with the prime minister, the boys with the president.

Mizanur Rahman's story is the stuff of family legend. He began his working life as a banker, but after rising rapidly up the ladder, he decided banking was not for him. Shortly after the bloody, convulsive war that led to Bangladesh's becoming independent in 1971, he decided to go it alone. He handed in his notice and began to import tires and inner tubes. From the start he did business on a simple principle not often followed in Bangladesh: if you borrow money from the bank, you pay it back. In a country with one of the highest default rates in the world, Mizanur Rahman was a good risk, and the banks wanted to lend money to him. That would help him later when he needed cash to begin the expansion that would create an empire.

Soon he moved on from tires and began trading in corrugated steel sheets. It was a good business move. In the seventies, Bangladesh was a country of mud huts thatched with straw, but change and a prosperity of sorts were coming. Slowly, people were starting to build their homes from corrugated steel. It was seen as progress, a way to prove that your family had made it, and the potential customers could be counted in the tens of millions. The big cost in making corrugated steel was the raw material: steel.

Ship-breaking was just getting under way—it was the new way to get steel—and Mizanur Rahman decided he wanted a part of it. He acquired a section of the beach in 1982 and began his operations. From there, adding offshoots to the conglomerate had been a matter of logical progression: more sophisticated mills to process the steel, and factories producing the gas and oxygen to supply his own yard and the rest of the ship-breaking industry. It was a time of expansion.

Now that Mizanur Rahman is in his sixties he is gradually letting go of the reins. Although he remains overall boss and chairman of the group he founded, he's passing on the responsibilities of its day-to-day running to his sons. Mohammed Mohsin is the oldest, so he's the first to be tested.

At the age of twenty-six, after studying in the United States, Mohammed had returned to Bangladesh. His father had called him into his office and told him that he was to be given ownership of a share of the family conglomerate, and that the ship-breaking arm of the company was now his responsibility to run. "I didn't sleep for six months," says Mohsin when recalling the pressure at such a young age. And soon he learned a hard lesson. Trusting a man the firm was doing business with turned into a mistake and Mohsin lost a large sum of money. When he admitted it to his father, Mizanur Rahman's response was to pull out a ledger recording the deals that had gone wrong for him over the years. Soon Mohsin grew into his role.

The pattern was followed as other brothers came of age and were given shares in PHP and a part of the firm to oversee. Mizanur Rahman's family grew in size along with his fortunes, and he now has seven sons, as well as one daughter. There are plenty of divisions of the firm to go around. Mizanur Rahman can afford to be content as he is driven home at the end of the day.

Like many families, Mizanur Rahman's clan live together. It is traditional in Bangladesh for sons to stay at home with their parents. On marriage their wives move in, too. In poorer families, who have cramped living quarters, it often leads to difficult relations between daughter-in-law and mother-in-law. The rich can afford to spread out a bit. Mizanur Rahman's family home is still on a relatively small plot, though, in the suburbs of Chittagong. It's on a hill slightly raised above the town, and the road that leads to it is potholed. The property is surrounded by a high wall, and the gate is guarded by men in military-looking uniforms who cradle old bolt-action rifles. The small concrete courtyard is crammed with the family's Land Cruisers and a single BMW 3 Series. On one side is a grand doorway into the building. It's flanked by pillars, but that isn't the way in. Instead, for now, visitors must walk past a prayer room on the ground floor and duck through a low entranceway that has been roughly bashed into a wall. The family has been living like this for months while workmen are in.

The doorway leads directly onto a concrete staircase. The house is only a temporary arrangement and inside, in places, it looks like a building site. The family is busy constructing an apartment block for themselves on the plot and the one next door. But in the meantime they are making do.

As the eldest son, Mohammed Mohsin has a suite of rooms on one of the upper floors. It is very basic. The living room, where he and his wife greet guests, has no furniture in it at all. Everyone sits on thin cushions laid out on the floor. The only other objects in the room are a large air-conditioning unit and a clock on the wall. Beyond the living room, a narrow corridor leads to a small dining room, where Mohsin's immediate family has breakfast. It is barely big enough for the table that's covered in a plastic sheet. On the walls Mohsin's two small children have used their crayons to scrawl the letters PHP. It shows an early enthusiasm for the firm that one day they may have a part in running.

Often the family eats upstairs in the apartments where Mohsin's father lives. The rooms there are much grander, filled with heavy, ornately carved modern wooden furniture. Every evening, the cooks in the house make enough food for more than a hundred people. It is a matter of pride for the family that everyone eats the same thing, even the house servants and the drivers. It's always traditional Bangladeshi food—rice and dhal, fried fish and vegetables, and lamb and chicken curries.

Mizanur Rahman and his eldest son are alike in many ways. They have the same broad grin in a round face and the self-assurance of rich men. They are also very different. Unlike his father, who claims to have no need of money, Mohsin has an unashamed love of cold, hard cash. He is spending $20,000 converting the Hummer he just bought from left-hand drive to right-hand drive. He also has plans to upgrade the interior with televisions and other gadgets. He confesses that he looked seriously at Vertu cell phones on his last trip to the Middle East. The platinum and jeweled sets are sold on the slogan that they are worth more, gram for gram, than twenty-four-karat gold.

Both father and son are the products of their upbringing. Mizanur Rahman is proud of the village he grew up in, and he still supports the people there, contributing to the building of clinics and schools. His values were shaped in a Third World country, one in which the individual is considered to be less important, particularly if he is poor. A place where the sacrifices of the men in the ship-breaking yards are worthwhile if they provide the nation with the steel it needs. But as Mizanur Rahman grew older and became more committed to his faith, his son was out seeing the world.

Mohsin attended college in Boston and speaks English with a slight American accent. He believes in the Western values of treating his employees as well as he can. But few who studied alongside him in American classrooms could imagine the scene on the beach where their friend now makes his living.

Mohsin is married to an American woman, Fabiana. Fabiana's family was originally from Thailand, but she spent her childhood in the United States. Like everything in Mohsin's life, she embodies the compromise between East and West. Fabiana has adopted all the ways of a Bangladeshi woman. She wears a traditional *shalwar kameez*, dotes on her father-in-law, and says that she is so happy in Bangladesh that she has all but forgotten her parents back on the other side of the world. In the evenings, when there are guests in the house, she dutifully dishes out the food at the table onto each diner's plate.

As his daughter-in-law goes around with the dishes of rice and curry, Mizanur Rahman expounds upon his beliefs. His son listens respectfully. The patriarch dominates the conversation with his mantras.

"The road to success is always under construction," he says echoing words he must have spoken to Mohsin as he was growing up, drumming in the value of hard work to a boy who had been born with privilege, a member of a wealthy family living among millions in poverty. Those riches were built in part on the backs of people who were willing to work very hard for very little.

Environmentalists and groups like the International Labor Organization have expressed deep concern about some of the ship-breaking yards along the beach: the danger, the poor pay, the working conditions. Mizanur Rahman believes that PHP at least is operating for the good of those who work there.

"Every human being is the most valuable thing," he says. "We're losing money, but that doesn't matter. Profit is not just money in the pocket but good for society. All these people are taking their daily bread."

For little more than a dollar a man a day, Mizanur Rahman employs hundreds of people as beasts of burden, risking injury or death. But he believes he is doing them a favor. And in a way, he's right. Working in the breaking yards is hell, but being utterly destitute in Bangladesh is worse.

Cutters on top of the Asian Tiger

CHAPTER THREE

BREAKING UP

A t low tide, the blacksmith struggles knee deep across the mudflats toward the *Asian Tiger*, a hammer in one hand, a chisel in the other. The muscles in his shoulders stand out in ridges, honed by his work. To the men watching from the beach, he looks tiny as he approaches the ship. The hull towers above him. He reaches the bow and runs his hand over the red paint and the barnacles. His bare feet squelch as he searches for a hold. Then he strikes the first blow against the *Asian Tiger* with his chisel. Metal clangs against metal, and the noise rings through the ship, echoing in the empty tanks, transmitted from bulkhead to bulkhead. The result is almost imperceptible; it leaves a tiny dent on the vast hull, but it is the first step in the process that will tear the ship apart.

"Two hundred taka for that man," says Mohammed Mohsin, "A tip to bring me good luck."

Over the next three days, teams of men hammer out a series of holes a foot or so square around the hull. They are specialists in this work, men who travel up and down the beach selling their skills to the breaking-yard owners. Each time a new ship arrives, they are called in. The labor is hard; the steel plates of an oil tanker are several inches thick and each breach takes at least an hour to make. Everything has to be done painstakingly by hand because the hold of the *Asian Tiger* is still full of potentially explosive gases and the remnants of the oil that she had once carried around the world. It's far too risky to use the naked flames of the blowtorches. The hatches on the deck have all been flung open to let out the gas. The holes far below what was the waterline when the ship was a working vessel also help to ventilate the tanks and let the sea wash in and out at high tide. Later, the water will catch sparks and help to prevent fires.

A week after the *Asian Tiger* is beached, the government inspector comes. He walks around the ship and scrambles into the tanks, waving around a device that electronically "sniffs" the air. Satisfied after his tour, he writes out the certificate. The *Asian Tiger* is officially free from gases and safe. The real work of breaking her up can begin.

Being appointed the first cutter to take a blowtorch to a ship is not a task the men consider an honor. Even though the government inspector has declared the *Asian Tiger* safe, there is still a chance of an explosion. The cutters cannot be totally sure until they see a flame break through the hull without incident. The men are all gathered on the beach when the contractor points at Shamsul.

"You do it," he says.

Shamsul dutifully picks up his blowtorch and goes to do the job with the promise of an extra few hundred taka (a few dollars). Once he makes his way out to the ship, he puts the flame to the steel low down on the bow. The metal begins to melt, running down in short streams of gooey, red-hot liquid. Shamsul holds the torch steady as a hole begins to form. The cutters on the beach hold their breath. There is no explosion, and they begin to relax. Later, they join in the cutting.

The first thing the cutters need to do is to make giant eyelets

A string of men dwarfed by the Asian Tiger

The string of men along the Asian Tiger

all over the front of the ship. The holes are cut in the steel in pairs on either side of bulkheads, where they can bear a huge strain. It had been a good beaching, but the *Asian Tiger* still needs to be closer to the high-water mark. Gangs of laborers gather by the three winch houses on the beach, where those who are wearing sandals kick them off. They are cheap plastic flip-flops that cost just fifteen cents or so in the market, but these men are poor and don't want to damage them if they can help it. The thick steel cables that run from the winches are twisted and coated with mud. Sharp bits of metal poke out. But as each cable is unwound from the drum and played out, the men join the line, taking the weight onto their shoulders. The teams stagger against the cables' stiffness as they heave to straighten them out. They struggle down the beach and out onto the mud in a long line, like pearls on a string, each bearing the weight of five meters or so of cable.

As the men make their way toward the *Asian Tiger,* the ground is sometimes firm damp sand under their feet, making walking easy. Other times, the men step into glutinous mud, formed from silt swept down the Ganges and Brahmaputra from the plains of northern India and the highlands of Tibet. Then the weight of the steel ropes presses the men down until they are knee and thigh deep in the sucking mess. Still they struggle out toward the *Asian Tiger*. It is low tide, and the entire front half of the ship is out of the water and resting on the mudflats. Her faraway stern is still in the sea.

Other laborers have already been busy on the ship. Tons of water have been pumped into the tanks near the bows to balance the ship. Empty of her cargo with her ballast shifted, the *Asian Tiger* had been heavily weighted toward the stern, where her mighty engine still sat. That was good when the ship was run aground, but it would have made it much more difficult to drag her farther up the beach.

The teams also attached smaller steel cables to the eyelets

that the cutters had made in the bows. In turn, each steel cable was joined by a system of pulley wheels to the thick steel cables that stretched back up the beach to the winch houses. By the time the men finished, the ship was tethered all over her bow. The three main cables from the winches were joined to four smaller ones so the strain was spread over twelve points on the ship. The arrangement was similar to that of the strings on a parachute.

Every one of the winches is a triumph of engineering in its own way, built with ingenuity and kept going with loving care. The winch drivers sit on ancient chairs with stuffing coming out of the seats; the rusting legs of the chairs are mounted in tubes soldered to the floor, a precaution to keep their occupants in place despite the tremendous vibration when their machines are at full strain. The diesel engines that power the winches are salvaged from crashed trucks. A throttle, a clutch, and a gear stick have been skillfully made with scavenged pieces of metal.

Once each of the engines begins to run smoothly, its driver kicks in his clutch, pushes the machine into gear, and guns the engine. Black smoke pumps into the sky and the winches begin to turn, drawing the steel rope taut. The sinister wail of an old air-raid siren fills the air, warning the workers to stand clear.

The carrying team hurries back through the mud toward safety. The more experienced men on the beach are the most concerned and draw back the farthest. It is the new arrivals who stand around nonchalantly, ignoring the risk of the steel cables snapping. If one breaks, the frayed ends can whip violently through the air, suddenly free of the immense strain they were under. That recoil is powerful enough to take off an arm or a head, or even to cut a man in half.

For two days the winches strain and roar, and the *Asian Tiger* is dragged slowly and ponderously over the flats, one inch at a time. Just a few weeks before, her progress had been majestic— she had created a mighty bow wave of seawater as she powered

A young worker

Chief cutter Mohammed Yunnus

through the ocean. Now all that is building up under her hull is mud. As the weight of silt being dragged along gets heavier, the work becomes harder and harder for the winches. Eventually, the contest becomes unequal and the machines can move the ship no farther. They subside into silence.

More eyelets are cut into the bows of the ship. The men struggle out into the mud again and add two more steel ropes to the end of each cable. Now the *Asian Tiger* is attached to the winch houses by ropes at eighteen points so more force can be exerted. For another straight day, the winches turn and the ship is pulled toward the beach before, at last, the men are satisfied she can come no closer. They had dragged the thirty-eight-thousand-ton vessel perhaps a hundred yards across the mud. Now, at low tide, the ship is clear of the water from bow to stern. The work of breaking her up will be easier, quicker, and, because of that, much more profitable.

Mohammed Mohsin is in a good mood as he visits the beach to see how progress is going on the ship. The *Asian Tiger* is safely on the beach, and he's already eagerly anticipating the profits. But this is still a risky time.

"What are our worries?" he says. "Explosions. We don't want a fire, but we have experts here who can smell dangerous gas. The heat of the summer also creates gas in there. Even though it's been certified gas free, it can still make gas."

There is a hierarchy in the ship-breaking yards, and the cutters who work on board the vessels are at the top. They are the skilled butchers who dismember the ship. It is a dangerous job, learned at the shoulder of a more experienced man during years of apprenticeship. The cutters' badges of office are their gum boots and faded boiler suits, printed with the logos of half the shipping lines of the world and scavenged from the lockers of vessels that passed through the yard earlier.

As they walk down the beach past the ragged laborers to

board an old lifeboat bobbing in the high-tide shallows, the cutters for this job wear sunglasses against the glare of the sun, and hard hats. The old diesel engine roars deafeningly as they make the short crossing to the *Asian Tiger*.

Mohammed Yunnus is a modest man, but he is the most senior cutter on the beach. After twenty-four years breaking ships, and a few before that building them overseas, he is the most experienced of the entire team. His job is the best paid: leading the cutters on board and overseeing the dismembering of the vessel. Yunnus is the first of the team to scramble up the rope ladder, the first through the hatch cut into the hull of the ship about twenty feet up. He ducks his head as he steps into the dark interior of the *Asian Tiger*.

For level after level, the tanker goes up, walkways and platforms linked by iron ladders and divided by bulkheads. In scale it is like a steel cathedral, and it feels as solid. The smell of oil is still strong; every surface is blackened. Shafts of sunlight come in through slashes cut into the hull, but it still seems dingy, the treacherous holes in the floors difficult to spot. Seawater mixed with oil glints far below, and the men pick their way through cautiously.

"When I first came in here, my heart pounded like this," whispers Mohammed Osman, the young cutter at the back of the line of men, pumping his fist rapidly. "It seemed very dark and as if the gas and oil could catch fire at any time. I was panicked."

On the deck, teams of workers are already removing the massive pipes that once carried the oil in and out of the hold. They are valuable and are being taken apart as they were put together, joint by joint. The workers unscrew the nuts and hammer out the foot-long bolts with sledgehammers. They use rods to work at the joints, forcing them apart. The joints have been sealed for more than twenty years and are stiff. Shiny black oil leaks across the deck. The pipes are carried to the bow of the ship and

Even the dregs of oil in the Asian Tiger *are saved for recycling*

Mohammed Yunnus at work

heaved over the side to land in the shallows. At low tide, teams of men retrieve them from the mud and carry them over their heads and away up the beach to be sold. Even the big old rubber washers from each joint of the pipes are salvaged.

It doesn't take much equipment to break up a ship on a beach in South Asia, just blowtorches and a continuous supply of cylinders of gas. The principle is to cut off large sections of the vessel that can then be dragged to shore by the winches and broken into pieces small enough to be loaded onto trucks and driven away.

Each cutter has a helper. His job is to ensure that the rubber hose to the gas cylinder is kept clear of snags. Sharp edges of steel can tear it. When the gas is turned on, the brass blowtorches hiss loudly. The helper lights the gas with his cheap plastic cigarette lighter and the blue flame whooshes.

With endless patience, the cutters apply the flames to the steel plate in the hold, trying to cut along the original joints from when the ship was built, ignoring the heat and the fumes. They begin with the ship's water tanks, giving the gases more time to disperse from the sections that had held oil. The ship is to be cut into L-shaped sections made up of chunks of the hull and the sides of the ship, around sixty feet by thirty feet in size, with the corresponding piece of the deck still attached.

Soon the ship cutters are getting ahead of the men on the beach, working too fast for them to keep up. A blowtorch cuts surprisingly quickly through plate steel, melting through a foot every couple of minutes. The steel sections are not cut free of the ship immediately. As each becomes almost completely detached, the men stop, leaving the last cuts that would cause the section to crash down until later. All along the ship, pieces of metal weighing hundreds of tons are held in place with ringbolts and a few remaining slivers of steel.

As space is cleared on the beach, the steel sections are cut from the ship one by one. Rather like felling a tree, when cutting a ship apart it is crucial to break through the correct bit last so that the section will fall safely outward and not inward, where it can crush the men. As the most senior cutter, Mohammed Yunnus often does this job. He goes down into the hold while the men gather on the deck to watch. There is no drama. There are no shouts and no warning as the piece of the ship begins to fall toward the sea. Its passage through the air is marked by a shower of black dust and dried oil. The sections are so huge they seem to move slowly before landing in the shallows with a boom. The white seawater splash reaches up higher than the deck, a hundred and fifty feet or more. Yunnus blinks in the sudden sunlight, a tiny blue flame still jetting from his blowtorch. The latest steel section severed from the ship settles its weight into the mud.

All day, every day, the beach rumbles at intervals as the giant pieces of steel fall from the ships. The breaking yards are spread along ten kilometers of the muddy, oily sand, and the work never stops. The winches roar as another giant section of ship is dragged through the mud. The strain increases as the steel moves up toward the beach. The edges dig in, picking up tons of mud, and the winches have to fight against the resistance.

Most of the pieces come to rest on their sides after they are cut from the ship, lying with what had been the outside of the hull facing downward. Pieces of metal that had once formed the deck are now vertical. Men clamber over the bulkheads, the ribs of the ship, and begin to shovel out the oil waste that is still lining what was the inside of the hold. That too will be sold, loaded into drums and taken away to be cleaned and used again. Not just the steel is being recycled.

Mohammed Afsa is standing at the base of a huge chunk of steel, his blowtorch setting off bursts of flame as the oil in the tank catches light. The L-shaped section towers forty feet or more above him. It has been cut from the *Asian Tiger* and dragged up by the winches through the mud and onto the beach. His job is to

Cutters work at a different angle

Beach cutter Mohammed Afsa

cut it into pieces the size of a tabletop big enough to seat more than a dozen people, around four feet across and twelve feet long. He works hard, ignoring the sun and the heat.

"This fuel tank is profitable to cut, and interesting," he says. "On passenger ships the sections are small, so it's not profitable for the company because we have to make more cuts. We get more money for this work because we can get through more steel."

As he speaks, his blowtorch sets off a fire that spreads rapidly, smoke billowing across the beach.

"Run, run," the men shout and laugh.

One man's route out is cut off, but he stands and waits calmly behind the heat haze, smoking a cigarette.

"It's not that dangerous here. Because we are in open places we can usually get out," says Mohammed Afsa. "The people who work on the ship get more money because they are in more danger." Mohammed Afsa earns just over two dollars for a nine-hour shift.

The carrying teams are at the bottom of the hierarchy on the beach because they are the least skilled and, thus, the lowest paid. They are cheaper than a crane, and that's why they're employed. They wear ragged *lungis*, skirtlike garments made of a tube of material loosely knotted around the waist, their filthy shirts hanging baggy on their thin bodies, frayed at the shoulders from the rough steel. These are men who do some of the toughest physical labor anywhere, for around a dollar a day. For the most part, they are small men, short and skinny, their faces burned dark brown from spending all day out in the hot tropical sun. Almost all of them grew up in the poorest districts of Bangladesh, where childhood malnutrition runs at more than fifty percent. Chittagong is in a relatively prosperous part of the country, and, although by international standards most of the people there are desperately impoverished, few locals consider working on the beach.

Among these laborers, the foremen like Mohammed Abdul Hakkim are kings. Hakkim is in his thirties and wiry; the spaces between his teeth blackened with plaque are on show when he smiles, which is often. He wears the same dirty shirt and *lungi* as everybody else on the beach, but the difference is in his eyes; not only are Hakkim's an unusual pale brown, but they also hold hope. Hakkim employs the men who work under him. The contractor pays Hakkim by the ton of metal the men move. Hakkim then distributes the money among the teams as he sees fit. Hakkim is in his position of power because of his ability to find men to work in the ship-breaking yard. He gathers them on recruitment drives in his home district of Bogra, in North Bengal. It is the poorest part of Bangladesh, and the men flock at the chance to earn a regular wage, no matter how hard the work. Hakkim has a team of sixty working on the beach. He personally earns up to twenty thousand taka ($350) every month. It is fine money for anyone in Bangladesh, one of the world's poorest nations. Even the most senior civil servants in the land or middle managers sitting in the offices of international companies can not expect to do as well.

All day, Hakkim directs his workers, ordering about twenty of his men at a time to gather around the tabletop-size pieces of steel. Each lump of metal weighs approximately eight hundred kilograms and the workers have to psych themselves up to take the enormous strain. The foreman begins the chant.

"Maro Joray hey-yah, shobai millay hey-yah, agai chollo hey-yah."

The men reply in deep unison, "With force, hey-yah, everybody hey-yah, go ahead hey-yah."

Then they bend down, grasp the steel, and, with a great groan, heave it onto their shoulders. Some have a piece of rolled-up cloth to use as protection against the sharp edges that threaten to cut into their shoulders and tear their shirts and flesh. Then the

A carrying team in the rain

The monsoon makes conditions treacherous

men march up the beach under the terrible weight, swaying in step, side to side in unison, and chanting. With his free hand, each man clutches the elbow of the man in front of him. Their feet slip in the mud. It is a brutally hard way to earn not much money.

Every day, dozens of trucks arrive at the beach. They are brightly painted, often with a picture of the owner's dream on the tailgate: a fine house or a peaceful country scene far away from the ship-breaking yards; the Taj Mahal, the great shining white Mughal mausoleum in India, is also a popular choice. While the truck drivers and helpers sit resting in the cabs, relaxing with cigarettes and joking, the carrying teams stagger toward them with the steel. It takes an extra heave to lift the front of the plate onto a roller placed at the back of the open truck. The men strain to push it forward a few inches at a time, ducking out of the way just before they are trapped between the steel and the truck. They run around to the back of the plate, joining the others to push.

Mohammed Akbar Hossain's job is to stand in the truck and steer the steel with a rod. His bare feet dance out of the way, and he jumps clear when the steel lurches forward unpredictably, the truck shaking as its suspension takes the weight.

"If I'm scared I can't do this job," he says. "I have to keep my mind sharp. At any time, an accident could happen."

The trucks rock violently as they are loaded, the ancient springs straining under the huge weight. Bangladesh's road rules officially limit these vehicles to carrying five tons. This dictate is always ignored, and the steel is piled high. As each fully loaded truck leaves the yard, it passes over a weigh bridge. The amount is carefully noted down in ledgers as, ton by ton, the broken-up steel is driven away. The metal from the *Asian Tiger* is being scattered all over the country.

Even as the men begin to tear the bow apart, the crew quarters near the stern look much as they did when the *Asian Tiger* was a living vessel. The cabins still look occupied. The beds in the cabins still have sheets, though they are unmade. The bikini calendars have, however, mysteriously disappeared from the walls in the offices. Scavengers now roam through the superstructure. Dealers pick over the contents of the ship, inspecting the the furniture, looking at the cooking equipment in the drawers of the galley. Workers from the breaking yard make piles on the deck: fire extinguishers, hard hats, and life jackets.

Everything is going to be sold.

Carrying away another steel plate

Mohammed Mohsin at the auction

CHAPTER FOUR

SOLD ALONG
THE ROADSIDE STALLS

"Furniture, furniture," shouts the security guard, looking official in a brown uniform and peaked cap. The buyers come into the room in the office building at the back of the breaking yard and sit in the rows of plastic chairs. Their faces are shiny with sweat despite the fans whirring on the ceiling. They spent the previous day on board the *Asian Tiger*, wandering through the cabins, the bridge, and the storerooms, examining the desks, the kitchen equipment, even the old stereo the captain had abandoned in his cabin.

Mohammed Mohsin sits behind a table at the front, his yard manager at his side. This is to be the first return on the enormous investment he has made in the *Asian Tiger*, and he's smiling broadly. In his hand he clutches a sheaf of papers, each with the letterhead of a furniture firm and a pay order to a bank, a guarantee that they will produce the money if their bid is successful.

"Furniture Plaza," he shouts.

From the room comes a muttered reply confirming that the company representative is there and that they are still interested in making a purchase.

Mohammed Mohsin shouts the names of the firms one after another.

"South Asia Furniture. Sigma Trading Corporation. M/S Trading."

After each comes the bid in reply. Cell phones chirrup; the loudspeaker in the minaret of the prayer hall on the other side of the street clicks and then hums into life. The mullah begins to sing out the call to the faithful to gather for dusk prayers. No one in the room moves.

"Hey," says Mohsin with a grin, accusing a man seated on the windowsill to his side. "You're looking at the prices I am writing."

Everyone in the room laughs, breaking the tension. Finally Mohsin seems satisfied. The winning bid for the furniture is $30,000 from SS Furniture House, and the buyer comes forward to write out his check. Mohsin smiles. "Compared to the cost of this ship, this money is very small indeed," he says. "But it is still money to me. I value it, I respect it, and I love it. It is money, and all the small, small, small together becomes big."

The sale goes on into the evening. There are the generators, the ship's wiring, and all the tools. Even the old oil in the ship's engine is to be sold. The lots come up one after another, and everything finds a buyer. There is nothing on board the *Asian Tiger* that is not of value to someone. It will all be put to a new use.

After the auction, the dealers are given a week to collect their purchases from the ship. Workers from the recycling firms scramble on board the *Asian Tiger* and begin to rip the cables and fittings from the vessel. Even the wood and insulation from the walls of the crew quarters are torn out and taken away. The tougher goods, the fire extinguishers and the life jackets, are hurled over the side at low tide. They land in the mud with a smack, to be gathered up and cleaned later. At high tide, old lifeboats cluster around the ship, bobbing about in the shade cast by the huge hull. Ropes snake down from the deck as the more

Removing navigation equipment from the Asian Tiger

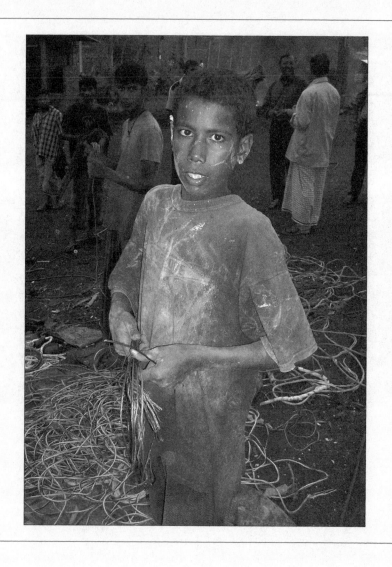

At work stripping cables

delicate items are lowered. It is a difficult operation, as the waves make the unstable lifeboats rock and lurch. But soon everything of value has been stripped out of the *Asian Tiger*. Her superstructure is forlorn and empty apart from the unwanted safety posters on the walls. In the bridge, all that is left is the vine that had once crept along the ceiling. Now its leaves lie on the floor, trampled. Week by week, the *Asian Tiger* is looking less like a living, working ship and more like a steel hulk. Soon there will be nothing left of her at all.

For mile after mile, the coast road behind the breaking yards is lined with shops selling everything that can be unscrewed and carried off the ships. Mighty electric generators, sufficient to power all the lights and equipment on a passenger liner, lie in the mud, alongside huge industrial cooling fans. Water tanks the size of cars are scattered about. Great blocks of concrete are piled up alongside the road. Once they were used as ballast; eventually, they will be taken from here and used to reinforce the banks of rivers, protecting towns and villages from Bangladesh's annual floods. Other shops offer radar domes, the stainless steel fittings out of ship's galleys, binoculars of every size. One specializes in workout equipment from gyms on board the ships. The exercise bikes and rowing machines stand in rows. Scrawny rickshaw wallahs stare at them as they pedal past, straining to move their machines laden with the weight of their passengers. The ships bring to Bangladesh products that might as well be from another world.

Everywhere, men are busily at work. Hundreds are laboring to break up pieces of metal. Deck railings are cut up with blowtorches. The smell of melting paint and the smoke hangs in the air. Farther along the road, a man smashes up industrial washing-machine drums with a sledgehammer. Others squat on giant cylinders from the ship's engines, chipping off the bronze bushes with chisels. The men do not know what will happen to the metal, only that every few weeks a buyer will arrive, load it all into a truck, and take it to India.

Teams of women are sitting among multicolored mounds of cotton waste, pulling the stuffing out of furniture too damaged to be resold whole. They use it to make thin mattresses.

It is here, by the roadside, that the contents of the ships are broken down even further to be sold. The town is the center of a mammoth recycling operation that has nothing to do with ethics or a desire to save the environment. It is prompted by the hard economics of need.

Wire is a big seller. Each ship contains around fifty tons of cables (passenger liners with their hundreds of cabins contain much more), and the supply from the breaking yards on the beach is enough to supply much of the local demand. It is used to carry electricity around houses and offices across Bangladesh. Some goes to repair cars. But few buyers want wires bundled together in cables several inches across. The wires have to be carefully pulled apart before they can be sold. Small boys do this job, and teams of them scramble over piles of cables outside the specialist wire shops.

"Only kids are interested in doing this work," says Abul Hossain, the contractor who has brought his young laborers to work here today.

He is sitting in the shade, chatting with the shop's owner.

"These boys came to me and asked for jobs, and now they are doing this work enthusiastically," he says.

The children drag the cables back and forth across a bamboo pole tied at head height between two trees to loosen the outer casings. The cables are stiff, having been installed on the ships twenty years and more ago. When the boys are satisfied with the progress, they lay the cables along the side of the road. Some of the cables are hundreds of yards long and zigzag back and forth in the mud. With a razor blade the boys slash the thick casing at one end, then walk back along the cables in pairs. One stands on the bared wires while the other heaves off the casing. The muscles in their thin arms strain. The smaller, more salable wiring within is wound into bales and thrown onto growing piles inside the shop. Every color, every diameter is available.

Shimon says he is twelve years old, but he looks younger. He wears a piece of bare metal wire as a necklace and a dirty T-shirt with "Virginia" emblazoned on the back. His sandals are far too big for his small feet.

"I'm doing this because my father married another woman, leaving me, my mother, and my brother," he says in a matter-of-fact manner.

His voice is not yet broken. He picks awkwardly at the glue that covers his hands.

"I earn sixty taka [$1] a day, and I am keeping the family. It's a big responsibility at my age."

Shimon has never been to school, and now he will probably never go. Poverty and hopelessness have been handed down from father to son in his family, just as privilege has been in other families.

In the evening, some of the wire shops burn the rubber from the casings, and thick black smoke billows into the air and across the road. Others dump it by the side of the highway, and it slowly sinks into the paddy fields. It will not rot.

The next day, Mohammed Badiul Alam sits in his shop made of corrugated iron. "In the next couple of weeks, I'm going to buy the tools and spares from another ship," he says.

His helpers, teenaged boys, are sorting through piles of needle-nose pliers. Tools and old bits of machines are piled on the shelves—here a heavy pneumatic drill, there a lathe—and laid out in front of the shack, protected from the driving monsoon rain by a tarpaulin awning. In the corner is a basket full of fire extinguishers; another contains dented tins that once held an industrial cleaning fluid. Alam is confident that he will find a buyer for it all. Someday a customer will come in wanting that spanner, the one that is three feet long with a head to fit a nut the size of a man's fist.

"It's a kind of gambling," he says, sitting behind his oil-stained wooden desk. "When the ships come we go on board to get an idea of what's there and measure how much profit we can make. I bought the hardware off the PHP ship for thirty-five thousand dollars, but sometimes I lose. I lost five thousand dollars about three months ago from a ship."

He shrugs.

"Profit and loss are brothers in business."

"I never make a loss," says Moazzem Hossain in his shop nearby. He has a hatchet face and smiles only when he makes a sale. He specializes in selling recycled polystyrene foam. The front of his shop is hidden behind a huge pile of it, thirty feet high. It had been torn from the holds of ships that carried chilled and frozen foods across the oceans. "I used to deal in engine parts, but this is a far better business," he says.

Hossain has a ready market. Hundreds of thousands of people along the coast are fishermen. They set out each day in tiny wooden boats into the often treacherous waters of the Bay of Bengal. Today, Anamdhar Das, a small wiry man with hands hardened by years of handling ropes, is giving his nets their annual overhaul. He came to Hossain to buy foam to use as floats.

"For these six bundles I am paying two thousand taka [$30]," he says. "We don't bother to bargain with the seller because the price is roughly the same everywhere. If anything, he's a bit cheaper."

The foam is loaded onto a flatbed bicycle rickshaw to be carried away, another small piece of a ship for which a new use has been found.

July and August are the peak months for the lifeboat dealers.

Fire extinguishers for sale

Piles of tins waiting for a buyer

It is the season for catching hilsa fish, Bangladesh's favorite variety, and demand from fishermen for boats is strong. Rafiqul Islam has sold twenty in the previous four weeks. He keeps the boats moored in the creek, near the sea, where they can easily be sailed out at high tide. When the water drops, the boats lie in rows, lined up along the banks.

"These two are the best I have ever seen," he says, slipping into his sales patter and pointing at the lifeboats that had once been on a container ship out of Mumbai.

MT Rajendra Pravan is stenciled on their bows in black paint. "Look, the engines have a gear system just like a car."

The seas, lakes, and rivers around Chittagong and across Bangladesh are dotted with lifeboats. They are used to punt families around Foy's Lake, the nearby beauty spot. Loggers come to Rafiqul Islam to buy lifeboats to drag tree trunks across lakes and rivers high in the forests of the hill tracts. The fisherman like lifeboats because they are made of fiberglass, which is easier to maintain and longer lasting than the traditional wood. Lifeboats don't need to be painted with pitch every season to keep them waterproof. The fishermen always go for open vessels, as it's easier to heave the nets over the side and haul in the catch. There is also a market for sealed lifeboats with roofs, used by seamen to survive in icy waters of the northern and southern oceans. They are good for carrying food and other cargo.

"The best thing about them is that they are all unused," says Rafiqul Islam.

He sells the boats for between forty thousand and sixty thousand taka ($600–$1000) and, like Henry Ford and his Model T cars, he offers only one color.

"What's the problem with them being orange?" he asks. "No one has ever complained."

All along the roadside, the dealers wait for customers, sitting behind wooden desks in their shops surrounded by their wares.

They smoke and chat comfortably in the shade, protected from the burning sun that scorches the laborers on the beach. Trucks and buses thunder down the narrow road that is Bangladesh's main highway, the link between the two biggest cities, Dhaka and Chittagong. Air horns blare as cars recklessly overtake each other, weaving into the oncoming traffic. Accidents are frequent. When they occur, crowds gather to admire the wreckage. The drivers of the delayed buses and trucks always refuse to line up and, instead, try to jump the queue by going up on the outside or inside. It often causes logjams, and the traffic can be stationary for hours. Sometimes the army has to be called in to push the trapped vehicles off the road to clear the way. The shopkeepers don't care; it means they have captive customers. The passengers from the buses have little to ease their boredom other than browsing.

Just twenty years before, there had been little built along the roadside, but the breaking yards on the beach spawned the stalls, and they had quickly grown into a town that was called Bhatiary. In Bhatiary, there are schools, mosques, and even a bank. Schoolgirls pick their way through the wares and the mud on their way to lessons in their blue-and-white uniforms, their faces covered with black veils. Men in flowing robes and beards sit upright on cheap Chinese-made bicycles as they ride to prayers five times a day. Off-duty workers from the ship-breaking yards sit around tea stalls gossiping, the customers on benches made of cheap planks, the owner cross-legged in the wooden, boxlike shop, busy tending to the kettles blackened by the fire used to boil the water. Piles of tins of condensed milk and packets of sugar line the small shelves. Bangladeshis, particularly those who earn their living by hard physical labor, like their tea strong and sweet. Cookies in clear plastic bags swing from nails.

Every day in the early morning and late evening, a fruit and vegetable market appears by the side of the road. Vendors arrive

Hoses will be sold

The foam seller (right) gets a customer

and sit on piles of produce on the back of tricycle rickshaws. The stall holders perch ten feet above the ground. The rickshaw wallahs strain to pedal the load. The produce is sold from large round baskets on the ground, the fruit and vegetables stacked into neat pyramids. Soft fruit like guavas are protected from bruising by leaves. Other merchants have sacks of red chilies, spices, and rice. They shovel them onto scales to weigh them out for customers. Shortage of space and enthusiasm to be the closest to newly arriving business means the market gradually inches out into the road. The traffic has to drive past slowly.

Bhatiary developed to cater to the needs of all its residents, the dealers and the breaking-yard workers, but the real business of the town by the roadside is selling on the bounty from the ships. Steel fittings out of the galleys are in much demand and there is a brisk flow of buyers through Rafique Uddin's shop. Yar Ali Khan runs a restaurant in Chittagong and comes every few weeks for supplies. He picks over the heaps of utensils. Pots and pans hang from the ceiling; there is a pasta maker that would look more at home in a trendy kitchen in New York or London than here; industrial-size meat grinders are scattered on the floor. Dozens of old microwaves are piled up in a corner. Every inch of space in the shop is used. Rafique Uddin sits on an old chair, a fan suspended from the corrugated-iron ceiling above him, two cell phones lying on his battered table.

"Everything here is good and cheap," says Yar Ali Khan as he pays for his selections. "This ladle is two hundred taka here [$3]. Now, in the market in Chittagong town I would have to pay five hundred taka [$8]."

Rafique Uddin stocks everything the restaurant trade could need. Outside, a crane is lifting a large stainless steel electric oven onto the back of a truck. Uddin has a variety of industrial-size refrigerators and freezers, the kind with five or seven doors. They sell well in the sweltering tropical summer. New, they cost thousands of dollars; now the asking price is just six hundred, and there is plenty of bargaining to be done. It all comes with a one-year guarantee.

"Every week I buy new equipment from the ships," says Uddin. "I am always trying to buy, at least five times a day." He considers himself to be a medium-size player. Like everyone else, he is trying to get bigger, buying and selling his way to a fortune.

Mohammed Kafiluddin is in his early twenties and is finding his way around the raw capitalism of the market on the coast road behind the ship-breaking yards. He set up his business a few months before with a loan of $6,000 from his family. He specializes in safety equipment. Outside the front of his shop are neat piles of fire extinguishers. Inside, life jackets swing from the ceiling. One shelf is covered with immersion suits, rubber outfits to wear to survive in cold water if shipwrecked. He has also taken some risks, splashing some of his start-up money on some unusual items. He is convinced he will find buyers for his fake Christmas trees in Islamic Bangladesh, in August. They stand out front under the hot tropical sun, bedecked in tinsel. The bottle-green clashes with the vivid paddy fields.

"They will sell well," he insists, persuading only himself. "Buyers from Dhaka will come here and purchase these trees."

The young shopkeeper's determined optimism is not necessarily unfounded. In Chittagong, there is a market for anything, and every item has its price. Here, even half-used bottles of toilet cleaner and opened boxes of breakfast cereal past their sell-by date are waiting for a buyer, and often find one. The labels are printed in the languages of the seafaring nations of the world. Sophisticated marine electronics that cost hundreds of thousands of dollars new are now on sale for a few hundred dollars. Much of the equipment is lying out in the rain in front of the shops, perhaps protected by an old piece of canvas. All will be snapped up and either put into another ship and sent off around the world again, or broken up for the parts or just to salvage the metal and plastic from which it is made.

When a ship dies on the beaches north of Chittagong, nothing is wasted.

A worker taking a rest

CHAPTER FIVE

MEN ON THE BEACH

t is late June, and the *Asian Tiger* is more than half gone. In just nine weeks, the cutters have worked their way back toward her stern. Her great bow fell into the sea long ago and was dragged up to the beach to be torn apart. The front of the ship now ends abruptly with a squared-off wound. What once was a bulkhead between the tanks is a steel cliff, and at high tide the water laps at its foot. Spidery-thin iron ladders crisscross up from the sea to the deck. Once they were used to give access to inspect the tanks; now they are the way the men from the breaking yard get on board.

No recognizable trace of the place where the *Asian Tiger*'s name had been proudly painted remains. The pieces are among the steel plates that have been stacked all over the mud in piles, each five feet high, the greatest height the men could heave the metal up to from their shoulders. The cutters are working faster than the metal can be loaded onto the trucks, so it has to be stored on the beach, turning rust-colored in the rain.

By now it is the annual monsoon season. The beach is drenched every day with torrential downpours, bringing more danger for the carrying teams. As they transport the steel plates up the beach, they stumble and slip through ankle-deep mud. Their hair is slicked with rain, and their thin clothes soaked. It is warm and humid, but in the early mornings before the sun is up and in the late evenings after it has gone down, the men shiver in the breeze that blows off the sea.

Mohammed Khokon's shoulders ache. He is still not used to the excruciating weight of the steel plates. He has been working in the ship-breaking yard for just a month, and his muscles have not toughened up sufficiently yet. Khokon is just seventeen years old, and his voice is husky one minute, squeaky the next. He has fuzz on his chin, but he's already doing a man's job. His body is crying out in protest.

One of Khokon's only possessions, and the one he keeps closest at night in case anyone tries to steal it, is a piece of rubber foam he scavenged. He uses it to cover the sharp edges of the steel to try to protect his flesh. But it is not enough, and his only shirt is stained with oil and dirt, and worn through on the shoulders. The skin that shows through is raw. The men who have been in the breaking yards longer have developed thicker skin on their shoulders, but that takes time and getting there is painful.

Khokon is standing and taking a rest in one of the winch houses, out of sight of the foreman and protected from the rain that drizzles down the corrugated-iron roof. His legs up to his knees are covered with dry mud. It is slippery today, and everyone on the carrying team is trying to be extra careful. They know it is dangerous. Despite the hard work and the risk, Khokon is glad he left Bogra, far to the north.

"Life here is better," he says.

At home, he claims, his parents had been cruel to him and, anyway, as for many families in the area, there had not been enough to eat. Along with the other young men of the village, he had hung around all day with little work and not much hope of finding any in the fields or the village shops. So when the fore-

Sheltering from the monsoon rains in the slum

man came, one who was looking for new men for the ship-breaking yards, Khokon had seized the opportunity to go, joining the others for the long bus ride to Chittagong.

Khokon was now earning just seventy takas (just over $1) for an eight-hour day. It was far better money than he would ever have got in Bogra, but still not much. "Rice is sixty-five takas [just over $1] a kilogram," he says. "And breakfast is so expensive too, it costs twelve taka [20 cents]." Khokon had come to the beach looking for a better future, but at a young age he has learned to dream small dreams. His life's ambition is not to be a doctor or an engineer or even one of the cutters in the ship-breaking yards. Instead, it is to own a cheap Indian-made motorbike.

Khokon is looking forward to going back to his home district. In poverty-stricken Bogra, the men who return from the breaking yards are considered rich; those with even a little money are looked up to by those who have nothing. And the villagers who have not been to the breaking yards cannot imagine what the men have been through to earn those few dollars—the stumbling through the mud, the agony of hours of lifting, submitting to the shouted orders of the foremen.

"Nobody from back home can see me doing this," says Khokon as he headed back to his carrying team to start work again. There is only so much time he can linger before the foreman notices he is gone.

"If I did a bad job, in my home district I would feel humiliated."

There is almost no chance of promotion in the breaking yard. A man who arrives as a member of a carrying team like Khokon is likely to remain one for the rest of his life, or until he manages to find a better job somewhere else. That's just the way it is, and everybody accepts it without question.

Azizul Haque signed up four years earlier and has been carrying steel ever since, working mostly at night. Now he is desperate to leave. He stands in the darkness of the beach, a basket made with bamboo and plastic sheeting on his head to protect him from the rain.

"This is a terrible job," he says.

Still in his early twenties, he had left his family in Purigram, in North Bengal, to move to Dhaka for a job in the garment industry. Like a million others in Bangladesh's capital, he had worked long hours making clothes, sweaters, shirts, and jeans to be sold in the West. Then the Chinese began to do the work more cheaply and the factory went out of business. The garment industry was hard work and paid badly, but it was better than the breaking yards, and ever since, Haque has been desperate to go back.

"I'm trying to get a job in the town of Comilla," he says. "I hope to go next month. I'm one-hundred-percent hopeful. I've got an assurance."

Haque says he would not be sad to leave the beach. "When I leave this place I'll be a happy man that day. Everybody wants a better job, but we have no options." Three months later he is still carrying steel.

Haque's chances of going back to the garment business are slim. The Multi-Fiber Arrangement is being abolished at the end of the year. For thirty years, the international system of import quotas has given the garment industries of developing countries like Bangladesh a slice of the market in the United States and Europe. It limits the amount of clothing China is allowed to sell. But with a new free market around the corner, Bangladesh's factories are already getting fewer orders. Some are closing, and those that remain in business will need to keep a closer eye on costs and recruit fewer staff. For Haque a better life remains elusive.

After their shifts in the breaking yard are over, the men troop through the metal gates of the yard, watched carefully by the security guards who monitor who's going in and out. The men

The line outside the cinema

gather in the tea shops along the mud road. Like almost all the buildings in the workers' village, the tea shops are made of wood and have corrugated-iron roofs. There are benches to sit on and rough-built wooden tables covered with torn sheets of plastic. The sides of the shops are open, covered just by a loose metal grille, and sometimes the rain blows in. But the tea served is sweet and hot, and made the way the men like it, very strong with condensed milk and lots of sugar. Tea drinking was brought to Bengal by the British and it has remained a passion. The shops also serve food—chickpeas in a spicy sauce, fried samosas and sringaras containing spicy meat and vegetables, and sweet fried pastries—but the men are not able to afford them often. The delicacies are prepared in great aluminum pots out in the street. Flies swarm around them, attracted by the easy meal. Bananas hang from hooks screwed into the ceiling. Small boys employed as waiters run back and forth with the tea in small cups and saucers.

The shop owners sit behind desks on ragged chairs and hold court with their customers. They stay there to look after the money, carefully tucking the notes and coins into a drawer and laboriously writing out a receipt for each diner. The little cash in their drawers is all in small denominations. Most of the owners have installed black-and-white televisions mounted on high shelves, and the men sit and watch the latest soap operas through the snow and fuzz on the screens. The biggest crowds are always drawn when Bangladesh is playing a cricket test match. Then the men who do not want to spend their money stand in the puddles and mud of the street and crane their necks for a good view.

The only other entertainment in the workers' village is what they grandly call the cinema hall. It is another small wood and corrugated-iron hut with wooden benches, but at the front there is an old color television linked to a DVD player. The walls are covered with black cloth that shuts out the light and the prying eyes of those who haven't paid. During the day, the cinema hall shows local Bangladeshi-made films; the sound of the violent fights on screen and the piercing singing of the heroines during the frequent dance scenes can be heard a long way around the village. The volume is turned up so high that the dialogue is distorted and can barely be understood.

Each film follows an almost identical story line. A hard man from the slum becomes a hero by leading a gang. Invariably, he takes on a rich and powerful man and wins, seducing his daughter along the way. It is escapism for men who will never get away from the poverty that brought them to the beach. They can watch a man who did make good, who took on the system and won. It will not happen to them.

In the evening, after sunset, the cinema hall owner puts on Western pornographic films smuggled into Bangladesh with other pirated DVDs from Pakistan, from the port at Chittagong and by plane. The owner warily watches for police at the door, as such films are illegal. But they're also popular and worth the risk, and officers can usually be paid off if they choose that moment to look around the village. There is always a line when such films are shown, and the price of admission goes up from seven taka to ten (eleven cents to sixteen cents). When the men cannot afford to go to the cinema, they hang around the streets, ducking under the corrugated-iron eaves of the shops when the monsoon rain beats down especially hard. This is not a living village with families and women and fun; this is a place men come to work and endure in.

Most of the workers stay in accommodations provided by the company because they can afford little else. Some are housed in the low concrete blocks at the back of the ship-breaking yards, two stories high with a balcony running the length of the upper floor. The single rooms each house several men, but they are usually the more senior workers like the foremen and the cutters.

The members of the carrying teams live in the long, low bungalows that are scattered around the village between the breaking yard and the coast road. The floors are made of mud beaten down by footfalls over the years. The walls are bare woven bamboo, and during the day the light shines through the gaps between the stalks. At night the mosquitoes fly in, carrying malaria and dengue fever, which the men call breakbone fever because of the extreme rictus-like pain it causes. The doors are made of rough wood and don't fit the frames. Outside there are puddles and mud left by the rain.

The buildings are about ten feet wide by eighty or so feet long, and are divided into small rooms by woven walls that are only head height. There are no ceilings, and the bamboo beams and poles holding up the corrugated-iron roofs are on show. If the occupants stand on tiptoes they can see down the length of the buildings. All day and night, whispered and shouted conversations are going on between the rooms. Each room is only ten feet square, but none of the men has one to himself. It is perhaps fortunate that they have few possessions to store inside, just one or two shirts and *lungi*s hanging over the beams, and maybe a kerosene lamp and a burner with which to cook. Some have a few pots and plates and a small store of rice. For drinking, there is the tube well outside, where they can draw up water with the hand pump. The men sleep on beds made of wood; the planks have not been sanded smooth and there are no mattresses. At night they simply lay out a *lungi* on the hard slats.

Thirty-year-old Mohammed Siddiq shares a room with four others so that he can afford to send home twenty-five hundred taka ($40) from his meager salary every month. He is one of the better-paid men on the beach. Chittagong and the village behind the ship-breaking yard is an expensive place; it would cost too much for him to have his wife and children living with him. Instead, he spends his life dreaming of the journey home.

"If I have money in my pocket, then I go," he says.

That happens once every two or three months.

This is how life is for the rural poor across Bangladesh. People live in little better than huts, and even then the rooms are crowded. Millions are away from home, scratching a living in the cities or the factories. Millions more have left the country to work abroad, laboring for a pittance in the Middle East and Southeast Asia, doing the jobs the richer locals no longer want to do. The only thing the men say they miss is female company.

"It would be better if we had women here, because then when we came back from work food would be prepared," says Siddiq's eighteen-year-old roommate, Farooq. "We could live a more comfortable life then, if you know what I mean."

The others laugh loudly at the euphemism, enough to wake Delwar, who is sleeping on one of the beds after working all night. Occasionally, some of the men from the ship-breaking yard go to a brothel in Chittagong on a Friday, the Islamic day of prayer and their day off from work.

Mohammed Yunnus is luckier. Every day after work, he hurries home to his wife and daughter. The yard's most senior cutter lives in a small bamboo house between the beach and the coast road. From there, you can just hear the sound of the trucks rumbling away with the steel he helped cut. The home is just a few hundred yards from the ship-breaking yards, but unless the wind blows to the northeast, there is no smell of the fumes and filth and it feels pleasantly rural. The tiny three-room building is shaded by banana and mango trees. Cattle low in the shack that leans against the side of the house and chickens take shelter from the driving rain under the low eaves. Ducks gambol in the puddles forming in the yard. Stepping-stones of bricks have been laid out in a herringbone pattern, so visitors can keep their feet dry as they approach the front door, but the stones don't help much. Every time it pours, the path becomes a tumbling stream. When it is dry, it is just wide enough for a rickshaw. Yunnus's hard work

Veiled schoolgirls in Bhatiary

has bought a modestly good life for him and the prospect of a better future for his children.

Yunnus's own father died when he was a child, so he knows how tough it is in Bangladesh without a good start in life. He never had the chance to go to school, and so he is illiterate.

"I had great ambitions when I was young, but I am from a poor family and I can't read, so I can't fulfill my dreams," he says.

He is giving his boys the opportunities he missed. In the photos proudly displayed on the walls of the house, the boys sit in their school uniforms. The snapshots were taken in a studio, and the painted background is of a grand house with an upstairs and a driveway and fountains in the garden—a house far bigger than the one the family lives in. Yunnus and his wife, Hosnay Ara, have high hopes for their sons.

"I don't want them to work as ship breakers or cutters," says Hosnay Ara, pulling the edge of her sari over her head as a veil. "They are going to school, and I would like them to work in offices, not as cutters."

Along with the photographs, the house is decorated with warning signs taken from the ships. On the back of the door, one reads "Fire Extinguisher" in English and Chinese. The walls are made of woven bamboo mats. The living room is sparsely furnished with a roughly made wooden bed and an old desk that they use as a dining table. It was painted institutional green long ago but has since been chipped and scarred by years at sea and hard use by a boisterous young family. A packet of Star cigarettes is on the lintel above the door.

"Lots of people build their houses of bricks," says Yunnus. "If I had the money I would do it too, but I'm the only earner in my family."

Seven people live on Yunnus's wages from the breaking yard. He supports his children, his wife, and his parents. The family's hopes—and indeed their very survival—rests on Yunnus's health, and he is employed in one of the most hazardous industries in the world, doing work that every year in ship-breaking yards up and down the beach costs men their limbs and their lives. There are so many ways to get hurt, including falling steel and explosions from the gases that remain inside the oil tankers. It is a perilous position.

"If I got sick for a month or for some days the process of earning and spending would be stopped," says Yunnus. "If it was something minor, I could borrow money from neighbors, but if I got a serious disease or was badly hurt, only God knows who would look after my family."

Hosnay Ara watches anxiously each day as her husband goes to work. She stays in the home and looks after their daughter, still too young to go to school.

"It's totally normal to be worried. I worry if he is okay or not," Hosnay Ara says. "He goes out in the morning and I wait for him to come back in one piece in the evening. It's very common; all the wives whose husbands work in the ship-breaking yards worry."

The cut-open stern of the Asian Tiger

CHAPTER SIX

HOW IT ALL BEGAN

An industry that provides work to a hundred thousand people and supplies Bangladesh with almost all of its steel began with an accident. The year 1965 was one of storms in the Bay of Bengal. One particularly violent tempest coincided with an unusually high tidal bore that swept north up the bay toward the mouth of the Ganges River. Some ships dashed for the safety of the harbor; others tried to ride it out at anchor. The master of one cargo ship was unlucky. His vessel ran firmly aground on the mudflats near the city of Chittagong. By the time the tide and the storm subsided she had been left stranded, well above the high-water mark.

The efforts to drag her off went on for weeks. The stricken vessel was still a relatively new vessel with years of potential working life left in her. The owners were desperate to save her if they could. They tried to pull her free with tugs, and they waited for the next peak tide, hoping that she could be refloated. She was stuck fast. Eventually, the salvagers had to admit failure. The ship became a curiosity for the local people. The children came to stare at the vessel high on the beach, out of the water. She would have rusted there had not the demand for metal in the area been so high.

Soon local businessmen saw the potential of all that steel lying on the beach and began to tear her apart. They took away the structure and anything else of value left on board. They stripped her bare and carried off everything. The premature death of the ship had been a stroke of good fortune for the people of Chittagong—she was an unexpected bounty from the sea—but no more vessels came to grief on the coast, and ship-breaking was forgotten for a while.

It took a war to get the industry going again. In 1971, discontent that had simmered for decades between what were then East and West Pakistan exploded into conflict. The two territories had been joined together after the British left, despite being separated by more than a thousand miles of India. Their only link was the common Islamic faith of their people. It had always been an uneasy union and it broke apart after the government in West Pakistan refused to cede control to Sheikh Mujibur Rahman, the nationalist leader who had won enough seats in Parliament from the East to form a government for the entire country.

At first the war was an unequal struggle, rebellious regiments from the East and peasants with old rifles against the bulk of the Pakistan army from the West. The Pakistani crackdown was ferocious and everywhere there was killing and raping and destruction. Nearly ten million refugees fled across the border. India, which had already fought two wars against Pakistan, trained and equipped the Bengali fighters, who became known as the Mukti Bahini or Liberation Force. They attacked Pakistani Army bases from hideouts on the Indian side of the border. By December the Pakistanis were losing badly and declared war on India. That was a mistake. The Indian Army moved quickly into East Pakistan. One of the targets was the shipping in the Bay of Bengal.

The fighting had lasted for nine months before it ended with victory for the people of the East. It was agreed that East Pakistan would be allowed to break away, thus creating a new nation,

Bangladesh. But the war had destroyed the country's infrastructure, and the first years of independence were marked by famine and disorder. Just one of the myriad problems facing the new government was what to do with the crippled ships in the Bay of Bengal, the detritus of the conflict. They were blocking the channel to the port at Chittagong and impeding trade the country badly needed to get back on its feet. Two vessels, the *MV Al Abbas* and the *ST Avlos*, were towed to the beach north of the city, and it was decided that they should be sold off at auction. There was only one bidder.

Shirazul Islam Chowdhury was casting around at that time for a new business venture. He had been one of the richest men in the old East Pakistan, owning a large company specializing in jute production. The fiber, produced from plants related to hemp, is widely used to make items like bags, and is an important export from that part of the world. Shirazul Islam's firm controlled a large chunk of the market. But the government of independent Bangladesh was intent on imposing an interpretation of socialism on the new country. It was a disastrous policy that would lead to widespread hunger and the deaths of millions of people. Another of the casualties was Shirazul Islam's business. The firm the family had built up from scratch was abruptly nationalized. Shirazul Islam was not paid any compensation, but he was offered a job as an employee in the factory like everyone else. He was a proud man and turned down the offer, deciding instead to start afresh. The ships were the opportunity for which he had been waiting to rebuild his fortunes.

However, even Shirazul Islam's family doubted the wisdom of his big new idea. "We were cursing him, we called him a madman," recalled his son Zafrul Islam Chowdhury, who was a teenager at the time. "'What are you doing?' we said to him. You might as well put the money in the sea."

Shirazul Islam paid around eight million taka (at the time

about $1 million) for the ships. The government was not willing to let them go for a complete song, although it did throw in the use of the stretch of beach where the ships had been dumped as part of the deal. Shirazul Islam bought some adjacent land to give him more space to set up his new operation. Everyone in Chittagong waited to see what he would do with his new acquisitions.

Shirazul Islam had a hunch he could make a profit on the ships by breaking them up. They were made of valuable metal, by weight worth more than he had paid. Turning the metal into a salable form was difficult, though, and no one knew how it was to be done. Finding the answer would be a case of trial and error. The work proceeded painfully slowly, and Shirazul Islam's family became even more convinced that they had been right all along. The money they had salvaged from the disaster of nationalization had been wasted.

Recruiting workers was not difficult. Those were the days when Bangladesh was described as a basket case by U.S. Secretary of State Henry Kissinger, because the country was devastated first by war and then by incompetent rulers. Millions of people were desperate for work of any kind, but few had any experience with ships, and none had ever attempted to break one up. The men began by simply taking the ships apart in the way in which they had been built, piece by piece. Vessels of the vintage of the *MV Al Abbas* and the *ST Avlos* were made of steel sheets held together by rivets. So hordes of workers clambered aboard all the ships, hammering out the little metal pegs one by one. The clanking was deafening and went on and on for week after week. The rivets were rusted in after years at sea, and it took a lot of work to free each steel plate. Then someone had the idea of cutting up the ship with blowtorches. That worked well, but the gas and oxygen needed to get a hot enough flame were in short supply in postwar Bangladesh. Shirazul Islam made a deal with the producers. He gave them for free the fire extinguishers from his vessels to use as canisters in return for a pledge to supply him with as much gas as possible. But still there was not enough, and when the gas ran out the workers had to go back to using the hammers.

Shirazul Islam quickly realized that the easiest way of breaking the ships would be to drag sections farther up to the beach, well above the high-water mark, where they could be dismantled properly on completely dry land. But the pieces were so heavy it was almost impossible for teams of men simply hauling on ropes to move them very far. So they scavenged cogs and wheels from the ships' engines and workings and made winches that were anchored by piles driven deep into the mud and sand of the beach. The machines were used to pull the parts of the ship farther up the beach on steel cables. They were geared so that they could be turned by muscle power alone. The work began to proceed more quickly.

There was still the problem of finding customers. The company needed someone to buy the metal, and in those days not many people in Bangladesh wanted old steel plates. They were quite simply the wrong shape. All steel being used in the country then came in the form of large sausage-shaped ingots. The factories and mills were designed for only the one size. The metal from the ships came in flat plates of lots of different shapes and sizes, and would not fit. Shirazul Islam's solution was to build his own rerolling mill that could cope with the metal from his vessels. He designed a process by which the steel was melted down and converted it into ribbed reinforcing rods that could be used by the construction industry to strengthen buildings made of poured concrete. He even managed to save some money by using the diesel and engine oil in the ships as fuel to fire his furnaces. It was dirty and filled the air around his mill with black smoke and a bad smell, but it certainly kept the costs down.

As the teething problems were solved, it quickly became clear that the ship-breaking business would be immensely profitable. There was no real competition. A state-run mill was the only other provider of steel in Bangladesh. Shirazul Islam could provide the same product much more cheaply and still make lots of money for himself. For the weight of metal they contained, the ships had been a bargain. As the last few pieces of the *MV Al Abbas* and *ST Avlos* were dragged away from the beach and melted down, Shirazul Islam headed to Singapore and bought three more ships.

There were the bureaucratic tangles typical of the Third World to break through, of course. Bangladesh's customs officials were not sure how to treat metal imported into the country in the form of working ships, but eventually they negotiated a solution satisfactory to all. Shirazul Islam had begun to rebuild his fortunes. He had also started a whole new industry.

Other businessmen in Chittagong were eyeing the handsome returns that Shirazul Islam was getting and began to scour the world market for old ships to break up, too. Nature had made their particular stretch of coastline ideal for the work. The sea rises and falls by six meters between high and low tide. At some times of the day, the water comes right up to the top of the beach, but at low tide a belt of mudflats at least a quarter of a mile wide is exposed. For most of the day, even the biggest ships run aground there would be completely out of the water. Companies were formed and agreements reached with the government to lease sections of the shoreline. Within a few years, a coastal belt some ten miles long was filled with ships in varying stages of being dismantled. Mohammed Mohsin's father, Mizanur Rahman of PHP, had spotted the opportunity, and had begun his own operations. An industry had been born, but at a heavy price to the workers and the environment.

Until the 1970s, ship-breaking had been carried out with cranes in sophisticated and highly mechanized dockyards in Europe and the United States. It was done in a controlled manner, with at least some care taken to ensure the safety of the workers and to protect the environment. Even so, it was a dirty industry, and as Western countries got richer they did not want it taking place on their coastlines. The regulations governing how ships would be dismantled got stricter, and it became more and more costly to comply with them. Eventually, simple economics finished the industry in the West, and ships went to more distant shores to die.

Ships have a lifespan of twenty-five or so years before the cost of insuring them and their cargoes renders them unprofitable to operate and they must be scrapped. Shipping is a cutthroat industry with narrow margins. The value of the steel in a ship at the end of its life is usually the difference between profit and loss for its final owner. In Western countries, the cost of scrapping a ship had begun to exceed the price that could be obtained for the metal. Ship-breaking had to move to places where the lives of workers were considered cheap and little value was placed on the environment.

Soon, most of the world's ships that were deemed to have passed their sell-by date were ending up on the beaches of India, Pakistan, and Bangladesh. There, the breaking-up process is much more simple and profitable. The ships can be run ashore and torn apart by men with their bare hands. Few employers offer any form of safety equipment. Often there are no gum boots, no overalls, and no eye protection for men using bright cutting torches all day. Workers die in explosions in the dark holds of vessels as gases ignite. Others suffocate. If steel plates are dropped as they're carried up the beach, men lose legs and arms or are paralyzed. It is not an unusual sight in Chittagong for men who have lost limbs breaking up ships to return to the beach to beg a living from their former colleagues. The workers give generously, hoping to avoid the same fate.

Other threats to the men's health are more insidious. Modern ships are ninety-five percent steel. Among the remaining five percent is enough dangerous materials for environmental groups to want waste ships to be labeled as hazardous waste. At Chittagong, these substances are released during the breaking-up process and make their way into the environment and into the bodies of the workers. When a team of environmental scientists from Greenpeace visited the area and took samples, they found asbestos littering the beach. There are high concentrations of oil in the soil and sediments, as well as heavy metals, mercury, lead, arsenic, and chromium, which can damage the nervous system. The air is regularly filled with the smoke from polluting fires as oil, plastics, PVC, and other unwanted substances are burned off. The men working on the beach and the people living nearby are being exposed to these substances continuously. The world's shipping industry and the fortunes of the yard owners rest on the men's willingness to take the risk of injury or death for just a dollar or so a day. South Asia, with its teeming millions living in dire poverty, is the perfect location. By the 1980s, the industry in Chittagong was booming, but there was still plenty of room for growth.

For the first few years, the men on the beach tackled only small vessels. The biggest they normally attempted weighed just five thousand tons, and that took six months to process. When one enterprising yard owner imported an eight-thousand-ton vessel, it was the talk of the town. For a month, people drove out of Chittagong along the coast road to stop and stare at it looming over the palm trees and paddy fields. The hawkers selling snacks and drinks pedaled their carts out every day and did a roaring trade.

Mizanur Rahman, the founder of PHP, was doing the same thing as everyone else who owned yards then—beaching small vessels and breaking them up. It was profitable, but he decided to

Ships lined up along the beach

The PHP section of the beach

take a big risk. In 1985, he bought and imported the first Very Large Crude Carrier to arrive on the beach in Bangladesh.

"It was the dream of all ship breakers to cut one up," said Mohammed Yassin Ali, another yard owner. Mizanur Rahman was the first to attempt it.

The vessel, which was very like the *Asian Tiger,* weighed forty thousand tons. It was a huge risk—no one knew if the methods used in Bangladesh to break up smaller vessels could be translated to such a massive ship, or if there would be sufficient buyers to make the effort worthwhile. But the risk paid off, and where Mizanur Rahman led, everyone else followed. Soon the beach was filled with massive tankers and passenger liners.

The leap forward for the ship-breaking industry coincided with a steep change in the demand for steel in Bangladesh. In the late 1980s, the then dictator of the country, General H. M. Ershad, was losing his grip on power. To try to maintain it, he initiated scores of building projects, hoping to prove his leadership was good for the economy. It did not save the general from a popular movement to restore democracy, but it did improve the fortunes of the ship breakers.

Ten years later, South Asia's ship breakers received another boost—ironically, from laws intended to protect the environment. In 1999, the *Erika* broke her back in the sea off France. She leaked ten thousand tons of heavy oil, polluting a four-hundred-kilometer stretch of the coastline of Brittany. Shortly after the disaster, the International Maritime Organization decided to phase out by 2015 vessels of her type, single-hulled oil tankers. They were thought to be too dangerous to be allowed to continue to ply the world's oceans. Then, in 2002, the *Prestige* sank off the coast of Spain, again releasing devastating pollution. Governments of the European Union agreed to ban single-hulled oil tankers from carrying fuels from their ports. The changes in the law meant the world's tanker fleet needed to be updated. It would take years, but in the meantime, efforts to protect coast-lines triggered by spills in Europe would mean good times for an industry that was polluting beaches in South Asia.

By June 2003, PHP was again testing its ambitions. The company bought and beached the sixth-largest ship in the world. The *Arctic Blue* was an Ultra Large Crude Carrier, an impossibly enormous vessel that normally stayed out in the deep ocean. She weighed nearly sixty-eight thousand tons and was by far the biggest ship that had ever been seen on the beach. They completely dismantled her in just five months, less time than it had taken twenty years earlier to process a vessel one-hundredth the size.

After that, the workers would be expected to make short work of the *Asian Tiger*, another single-hulled oil tanker, massive though she was.

The foreman, Mohammed Abdul Hakkim

CHAPTER SEVEN

IN THE
LAND OF THE POOR

Mohammed Abdul Hakkim knows he's going to need more men. The *Asian Tiger* was the biggest ship to have arrived in the breaking yard for a long time. She weighed thirty-eight thousand tons. It was a lot of metal, and all of it had to be carried up the beach and loaded onto the trucks.

The men will be busy in the yard for months, and that's an opportunity for Hakkim. He is the foreman of one of the carrying teams. He employs the men and oversees their work every day, chivvying and motivating them to move more steel plates, to meet the targets set by the contractor. He leads the chants the men sing out to build up their strength before each lift. But his position on the beach is guaranteed only by his ability to recruit sufficient workers to get the job done.

Fourteen years earlier, Hakkim arrived at the breaking yard from his home village in North Bengal, in the far northwest of Bangladesh. He had begun by working as an ordinary laborer in a carrying team, the lowest and poorest-paid position in the yard. For years he was one of the men who heaved the great steel plates onto their shoulders and swayed and sweated up the beach. All men found the work exhausting, and at the end of the day most did little but eat as much rice as they could afford to buy, and sleep. But Hakkim found the time and energy to plan a better future for himself.

"I came here under the supervision of another foreman and, day by day, I saved the money to become a foreman myself," he says. "You need three to four lakh taka [$5,000 to $7,000] to start. Now that person is working under my supervision."

Hakkim had never been to school, had no family money, and had no connections. He rose above other men by sheer determination. Hakkim is one of the few who have achieved their dreams on the beach.

Early in the morning, as the day-shift workers are just beginning to stir from their sleep, Hakkim walks away from the room where he lives in the concrete block at the back of the breaking yard. It is a few doors down from the contractor's office. He sets off by foot up the dirt track used by the trucks carrying the steel. It winds through the village that has grown up to house the workers from the breaking yards. On the coast road, he hails a bus bound for the district of Bogra. The vehicle is ramshackle and uncomfortable. The sides are beaten in by numerous bumps and crashes, and the paint is almost completely scraped off. Some of the dents have been covered with bare filler. It is hot inside, even with all the windows thrown open. The seats are plastic, and there isn't much legroom, but Hakkim is happy. He is going home for the first time in months. Hakkim lives a life of hardship on the beach, among the oil and detritus of the ship breaking, but back in North Bengal he is a man of wealth, influence, and power.

It is a long journey, six hundred kilometers, with the bus bounding over the potholes and bumps in the road. The driver swerves recklessly, and his helper leans out the open door, clinging on with one hand and shouting and banging the side of the bus with a stick to encourage slower vehicles in front to get out of the way. There are frequent delays when they approach towns and markets. Then the helper jumps down and berates other bus drivers and people loading and unloading rickshaws—they are scattered all over the road—and he tries to direct the clogged traffic. The towns are a noisy cacophony of shouting and banging as everyone attempts to drive through at once.

First the bus passes through the countryside around Chittagong. It is a relatively wealthy area, the industrial center of the country, and the paddy fields are interspersed with factories and mills. The roads are busy with trucks carrying goods to and from the port. Dhaka, the capital, is the halfway point. It is clogged with traffic and people.

Up to the Jamuna River bridge, the largest in the country, the roads are smooth and freshly resurfaced, but as Hakkim's bus approaches Bogra the tarmac gets worse and the potholes deeper. There are few private cars here, and not many factories. The shops have little for sale. In each town and village, there are more young men hanging around with little to do. Bangladesh's northwest is the poorest area of an impoverished nation. But that makes it a good place for a man looking for recruits for some of the toughest jobs in the world.

The last ten kilometers of Hakkim's journey are by tricycle rickshaw. They bounce down narrow dirt pathways built up on low embankments between the flat green paddy fields. Hakkim sits on the padded bench; in front of him the wallah strains at the pedals, his shirt sticking to his sweaty back. Everywhere in the fields there are men bent double, planting rice and hoeing. The concrete shops and houses of the towns, and even the more prosperous villages, have given way to huts made of corrugated iron and bamboo. People are fishing in every stream and pool. Children smack the water with sticks, hoping to stun the fish for long enough to scoop them into a pot. Others cast nets or set homemade basket-weave traps. Some have built fishing machines so they can work from the bank. First they tie big square nets to a cross of bent bamboo. They set up a pole on the bank and another across it, acting as a pivot. Then the net is mounted at one end where it can be swung out over the river and dropped into the water. The fisherman on the other side, raising and lowering his net, can keep his feet dry.

Hakkim passes a furious man dragging a pair of bleating goats to the house of the village watchman. He had caught them in his fields, eating the crops, and the owner would have to pay a fine to get them back. A small boy is crying hysterically and trying to pull the goats' leads from the man's hands. He is naked and wet, and had plainly been neglecting his job as herdsman and swimming in the river with the other children.

There are banana trees and coconuts, and bee-eaters flitting over the paddy fields. The air is clean and fresh, and everything is bright vivid green. It looks like a rural idyll, but living here is hell. Poverty drives men from this place to make a living in the dirt and danger on the beach.

Hakkim is an important man in the breaking yard. He is a king at home. His wife is waiting for him with his baby son, and his more distant relatives have also gathered to welcome him. There are invitations to all the neighbors' houses for dinner. Most of them—indeed the entire village—depend on Hakkim for the work he can provide their menfolk. There are few opportunities in Shariakandi, and without Hakkim and the breaking yards in Chittagong, many in the village would go hungry.

Hakkim does not have to look for workers; they come to him. They beat a path to his three-room corrugated-iron house as soon as word spreads that he's back in the village and wants more men. They gather to speak quietly to him as he sits on a wooden chair on the veranda.

Hakkim is a rich man. In a good month, he earns twenty thousand taka ($350), as much as a middle manager in an international company or the most senior civil servant. His house is

A fisherman

Abdul Hakkim in his home village

modest, but it is one of the best in the village. The only furniture inside is an ornate wooden bed and a plain table and set of chairs. The windows are covered by wooden shutters, and there is electric light powered by a solar panel. The floor of the house is bare earth; it has been swept over for years, until it is hard and smooth like concrete. The entire building is raised a few feet to give it some protection from the great wide Jamuna River, which flows languidly nearby. It is a wise precaution.

This year the entire district has been under waist-deep water and the farmers were forced to abandon their fields for months. A harvest was lost, and that only made the men of the village more desperate. In the evening, when Hakkim goes to the market where vegetables and the day's catches of fish are sold, the men spot him in the circles of light cast by the kerosene lanterns and approach him. Hakkim is taking just fifteen workers this time.

Zil Haq Hossain is desperate to go to Chittagong and the breaking yards. He is twenty-five years old and has never worked a steady job. Sometimes he gets a few days laboring, chopping, and moving mud, building up the banks around the paddy fields that keep the water at the right level to allow the rice to grow. It's hard work. Such workers use a spade to load baskets with earth and then hoist the baskets on their heads to carry them. Occasionally, someone asks Hossain to help with the planting or harvesting if it is a busy year. In a good month in the village, he makes seven hundred taka ($12), and he struggles to buy enough to eat. Often he's unemployed for days, weeks, or even months on end.

"If you want to eat better food, you can't without money," he says. "We eat lentils and fish—not big fish, the ones you can catch in the water of the paddy fields with a hook or a net."

If getting by becomes really difficult, Hossain goes south to Dhaka and joins the other migrants from the rural areas. The desperate flock to the capital in the millions, but there is little in the slums and the crowded streets for men like Zil Haq Hossain. He has no education and no skills. He often scrapes together money pedaling a rickshaw for a few weeks before heading back north. It is exhausting propelling the heavy machine through the busy streets under the hot sun, intimidated by the buses and the cars in the traffic jams, and there is harassment from the rickshaw garage owners, gangsters, and the police to contend with. So after a short while, he gives up. In the village, Zil Haq Hossain spends time sitting around or he goes to friends' houses for a chat. Sometimes he wanders along the paths through the fields. But most of all, he dreams about a better life. He thinks he might find it on the beach.

Hakkim has brought thirty thousand taka ($500) to the village with him. It is an enormous sum of money, more than most people in the village will ever manage to accumulate in their lifetimes. It is also a large personal investment for Hakkim, but he knows it will be worth it. He is offering recruits who sign up to go with him to Chittagong an advance of up to fifteen hundred taka ($25). The money will cover their families' living expenses until the men are paid and can start sending part of their salaries home. He is also paying for the bus ride down to Chittagong. It costs only three hundred fifty taka ($5.50), but most of the men cannot afford it on their own.

If his new employees wish, Hakkim will deduct part of the money from their wage packets every month until the entire advance is paid off. Then they can go to work for another foreman if they want. But few take this option and so they remain as indentured laborers, tied to Hakkim by bonds of debt, gratitude, and village loyalty.

"I imagine the work in Chittagong can't be that tough," Zil Haq Hossain says. "We gossip in the market with the workers when they are back here, and they tell us about the kind of job they have to do, carrying the iron plates. People from this village spend months and months down there, so it can't be that hard."

Zil Haq Hossain in North Bengal

Children of ship breakers

Zil Haq Hossain is tall and strong from digging the tough silt of the fields of Shariakandi, but Hakkim hesitates to take him on.

"Sometimes I lose money with new recruits," he says. "They might find the job too tough and quit. Then I have to count my losses."

The first few weeks of working in the breaking yards are always the toughest, even for men used to manual labor since childhood. It is the time when the muscles in the shoulders are still soft and the weight presses hard on the bones. Few men are used to carrying hundreds of kilograms on their shoulders. But Hakkim has a compelling argument to persuade those who wanted to give up, to stay.

"Remember the hunger in Bogra," he tells them. However hard the life is in Chittagong's breaking yards, few find the prospect of returning to nothing attractive.

The village relies on the men who go away to the beach. The population has grown larger over the years, and the problem of unemployment is getting worse. There is too little to do in the fields to occupy everybody. There are a few small sawmills, single machines powered by old diesel engines that were used to cut up logs into planks, but there is not much demand for planks because not many people have the money to buy them. One man makes a meager living by casting short round pipes in concrete. He pours it out of a bucket into the mold. The pipes are used as troughs to hold straw for cattle and goats. Some people run tea stalls or shops, but most have little to sell other than packets of cookies and bananas. Everyone else in the village relies on the remittances from the breaking yards. There are a hundred and twenty men from this one small village alone working on the beach. By scrimping and going without, most men manage to send back at least half their wages. A single earner can support a wife, children, parents, and siblings. In Shariakandi, two thousand taka ($35) goes a long way.

For months on end, the only contact between the families and the men away at work is through the cell-phone stall. A network of these stalls has been established across Bangladesh. In Shariakandi, it is a single Nokia handset attached to a wire that goes to an aerial mounted high above the trees on a bamboo mast. The people who work in the stall keep the phone carefully protected in a case. When not in use, it rests on a stand shaped like a deck chair. They watch it all day and answer it at once if it rings. All evening, every evening, people pop in to use it. Others hang around, hoping for passed-on news from their loved ones. Before the phone was installed, the previous year, the only means of communication was by letter. But many people can't read or write and had to get those in the village who could to help them. The mail was unreliable, and it often took six months for letters to arrive, if they got there at all. Almost all the calls from the cell-phone stall go to Chittagong.

Abdul Kallam has spent a month and a half in Shariakandi, and now it is time to go back to the breaking yard until next year. He has spent his time in the village relaxing, meeting up with old friends and family, and getting to know his children. His wife had given birth to another baby while he was away. He has also done the odd day of work, harvesting in his field of rice. But there has not been much to do. The floods have ruined this year's crop. A few years ago, Kallam had bought himself a third of an acre of land with the money he had earned on the beach. It was not much, certainly not enough to provide his family with enough to live on, but it was a real achievement and he is proud of it. In rural Bangladesh, ownership of land puts men in a different class, and no one in the family had had a stake in the soil like that before. In the breaking yard, Kallam is one among many workers, little more than a beast of burden, but back in the village he is a man of at least some status.

Abdul Kallam's cash is now on the point of running out, so

he has signed up again with Hakkim, the foreman, for another stint on the beach. He takes the advance and gives it to his wife. His adult life has been full of good-byes, of departures and returns. But that is normal in this part of the world. All the men who can, go away to earn money, and Kallam is looking forward to it.

"When we go there we can do some work and that's good," he says, bouncing his son in his arms. "I like being here, too, but we have to earn. The job is hard, but we know what to expect."

The men of Shariakandi have disjointed lives, a few weeks of leisure and pleasure in the village, followed by many months of bitter drudgery. They set off at ten o'clock in the morning, just as the sun is coming out from behind the clouds after a night of heavy rain, and the people of Shariakandi gather on the school field to say good-bye. The workers take few possessions with them, just a few *lungis* each and a couple of shirts. Most are carrying tiffin boxes of food for the journey, small stacks of tin bowls held together with wire that also forms a handle. They are filled with rice from the fields and a lentil broth called dhal. The men smile and laugh as they clamber onto the back of a small fleet of rickshaws and, waving, set off down the path, bouncing in the ruts. The children run behind them for a while, splashing in the puddles. The men are a long way off before the sounds of the bells on the rickshaws finally die away. Abdul Kallam's wife, Buly, turns back toward their home, their new baby in her arms.

"I've not seen the shipyards, so I can't imagine it," she says. "But sometimes he says to me, if you went and saw what the job was like, then you would not let me go."

The young Zil Haq Hossain was left behind to his dreams. With so few men going that time, it had been too much of a risk to take a novice.

A carrier on the beach under a homemade umbrella

CHAPTER EIGHT

THE BREAKING UP
IS NEARLY OVER

I t is the middle of August, the hottest month of summer and the peak of the annual monsoon. The rains come down in torrents, all day and night, and the puddles steam as the water evaporates back into the air, already overly laden with moisture. The men are soaked as they work; their thin shirts and *lungis* are soaked and stick to their skin. Their hair is slicked into spikes, and they shiver when the sun dips down toward the horizon at the end of the day. The mud underfoot makes carrying the heavy steel particularly treacherous. The teams abandon their plastic sandals and work barefoot to try to get a better hold, risking cuts and injuries from the sharp steel chips and discarded bolts and screws that litter the beach.

Steel plates have been laid haphazardly on the ground to try to make the pathways safer, but they are quickly buried in the glutinous mess and it's easy to trip over the edges. Each time the men heave the plates to their shoulders or take a step under the tremendous load, the uncertain footing threatens to send them tumbling. Every worker is muddied to the knee. This is the time of the year when accidents can easily happen, so the men are cautious and subdued.

The cutters on the beach keep dry by working under home-made umbrellas, which leaves them free to use their blowtorches. The men wear long, oval-shaped bamboo baskets lined with blue tarpaulin that covers their heads and backs as they crouch over the steel.

In just a few short months, the *Asian Tiger* has been almost entirely dismantled. At high tide, when the water reaches the top of the beach, it is now a boat ride to where the waves lap against what was left of the ship. That's an indication of the speed of progress; when she had been first driven aground, her bow had been left right up above the high-water mark. When the tide is low, the *Asian Tiger* is now stranded far out in the mud. In places, the flats are firm and sandy, and the children from the village play there, kicking around an old ball in endless games of soccer. Some of the boys have been hired by the cutters as gofers, and they rush back and forth across the flats to the beach with cups of sweet thick tea and lunches in metal containers that they attach to the end of ropes to be swung up the side of the vessel.

Much of the flats is a treacherous quagmire of mud where it has been churned and stirred by the lumps of steel as they're hauled from the ship to the beach. The silt washed down by the great rivers into the Bay of Bengal make it thick and goopy, and the men have to pick their way carefully, heaving to pull their feet from the sucking mud as they go out to begin their shifts, and when they return to the shore, tired, at the end of their work.

To the men, the achievement is commonplace, but the great vessel that had been impervious to storms at sea and had seemed indestructible is being torn apart virtually entirely by hand. The superstructure, where the crew lived and worked all those years as she plied the oceans between the Middle East and Southeast Asia, has been cut from the ship and dragged onto the beach. All the furniture from the cabins, the desks and beds and computers, went long ago, lowered on ropes and carried away. The machin-

Remains of the Asian Tiger, *stern to the left, bow to the right*

ery and controls that had enabled the crew to plot their course and steer the mighty oil tanker across the oceans was stripped out and sold, or donated to Bangladesh's navy.

The metal walls and ceilings of the accommodation areas have been torn apart by the cutters on the beach. Twisted and torn, some bits are still recognizable. There are safety warnings painted on one piece of metal that was a wall, and tiles still on what had been a bathroom floor, now lying at a crazy angle. On the beach, a showerhead and taps are recognizable.

The cutting teams on board have worked their way fore and aft through the hull from their starting point about halfway along. Now all that is left is the rearmost one hundred feet or so. Toward what was once the bow, the ship ends in a jagged metal wall with pipes and wires from the ship's workings visible. Men clamber among them. At the other end, the curve of part of the stern is still discernible, just, but it is recognizable only to those who had seen the ship when she was whole. The rudder that had been like an airliner's wing had gone months ago—torn off, dragged up the beach, and cut into small pieces like everything else. In the spring, she had been a living, working vessel, still at sea. Now much of the metal that made up the *Asian Tiger* lies in piles of rectangular steel plates lined up on the beach ready to be sold and driven away to the rerolling mills, to be put to a new use on land.

What remains to be cut up doesn't look like a ship. The *Asian Tiger* is now simply a large jagged lump of steel with the process of disposal almost finished. Her stern is splayed apart, as if the hull has been split by a giant can opener. One section on the side has been torn off, and it lies in the mud, still half attached. The white painted bulkheads and ribs of the inside of the vessel are exposed to the light for the first time since she was built. The drive shaft, which once linked the propeller to the engine, now ends in a roughly sawn-off stump. It is made of tempered steel and is the size of the trunk of an old and majestic tree. The great engine is exposed amid a jumble of pipes and cables, surrounded by taps and seals that no longer have a use. It is huge, the size and roughly the shape of a small house. The great engine block had a sloping top, like a roof, where the pistons had been mounted. Now the cylinders are empty, each big enough for several men to climb inside. The machine was surrounded by walkways that once gave access to the seafarers who had carefully maintained it and coaxed it through more than twenty years of journeys back and forth across the seas. Now the cutters are standing there inspecting the progress, deciding what to do next on this, the most dangerous stage of the process.

On ships the size of the *Asian Tiger*, the engine is never saved. There is no point; it is far too big for the ship-breaking yard to handle with the few single mechanical cranes on the beach, and there is no chance of transporting it whole along Bangladesh's clogged roads. Instead, it too will be melted down. A sophisticated machine that was capable of providing thousands of units of horsepower will become reinforcing rods in buildings like all the rest of the *Asian Tiger*. But before the engine is cut up, the men have to make sure there is no chance, even at this late stage, of a devastating explosion. Along with the great tanks that had carried the petroleum products that were her cargo, the ship had contained thousands of gallons of her own oil, used as a lubricant. At sea, the oil had kept the vessel's mechanics running smoothly; on the beach, it presents a real risk. The flame from a blowtorch could easily ignite the vapors—a devastating possibility in a confined space.

The cutters make a small hole by hand with chisels in the ship's hull near the pump room. It is a difficult and skilled task working out exactly the right spot, but the older men, like head cutter Mohammed Yunnus, have the knowledge of years of experience. They insert a thick hosepipe, and the dangerous black liq-

*At work on the beach—the supervisors use umbrellas
to protect themselves from the sun*

uid is sucked out and put into drums to be sold. Some inevitably escapes into the sea and joins the small slicks that dance in a kaleidoscope of color in the ripples of the shallows, but there is not much the men can do about that; ship-breaking is a messy business. The men are more concerned about whether the engine is completely clear. They wait until the flow of oil from the end of the hosepipes trickles to a stop. Then they wiggle the pipe inside the engine to make sure they've got every drop. When they are satisfied it is all out, the work of cutting up the engine and the metal housing around it begins.

The cutters scramble all over the lump of steel. Men work on ladders that lean up against the hull, making holes in the ship's sides. The metal is streaked with oil so that the steel is entirely black, and small flames catch light in the heat as it burns off. By now the original deck has been cut away, but it's still a long way up to the top of the ship's remains, forty feet or more. A rope ladder has been tied in place to give the men access. The metal rungs are slippery, but the men scamper up and down, ignoring the chasm below. Dozens of old ropes, steel cables, and chains also hang over the ship's sides so the men can lower down anything they find that's valuable. An old metal flat-bottomed barge lies in the mud alongside the ship, and it's filled with pieces of pipes and valves and small sheets of metal that had been cut away and salvaged. When the tide comes back in, the barge will be hauled to the shore, tied to the back of a motorized lifeboat for the items to be sorted and loaded onto the trucks. Bigger pieces of the ship's inner workings are lying discarded; a large, corkscrew-shaped pipe black with oil is half submerged in the mud—once it was part of a cooling system.

One of the ship's two giant boilers is being dragged up to the beach, with much protest from the winches. It a big box of corrugated metal with valves and pipes littering its outside, and its shape makes it dig into the soft ground, putting a strain on the cables. The other boiler is still on board, but it has been cut loose and is now at an odd angle. Soon it will be pushed into the mud, too.

Abu Taher is a cutter's assistant, and he is working on the underside of the *Asian Tiger*. It is low tide, and his feet in his old gum boots are planted in the mud outside the ship. There are puddles of oil in the footprints left all over the mud by the men walking to and fro. His head is inside the bowels of the tanker, poking through a hatch cut into the hull. He's standing where the flat bottom of the ship begins its curve up to the sides of the hull, and the great mass of steel looms over him. What remains of the *Asian Tiger* is stable enough in the mud that has held her firm these months past, but it looks as if at any moment the vessel could tip over, squashing Abu Taher flat.

The ship's insides are filled with an orange glow. Sparks from the cutting torches scatter among the pipes and valves and hatchways. The ship's remains are surrounded by acrid smoke, the smell of burning oil, and hot metal. Abu Taher is looking after the rubber pipes that carry the gas from the cylinders. He is making sure they don't get snagged.

"It doesn't make us happy that the job is nearly done," he says as he wipes the filth from his face with his gloved hand. "Any happiness is for the owner. What the hell is it to do with us? But it's going well."

One man who is pleased to see the job on the *Asian Tiger* coming to an end is Mohammed Mojibur Rahman. At the back of the ship-breaking yard, he heaves his portly frame up the old metal ship's gangway that has been recycled into the stairs to his office. It is a concrete room on the upper floor of the block where some of the foremen live, including Hakkim, who recruited the men from Bogra in the north. Rahman walks down the balcony that runs the length of the building to his door. From here there is a good view all over the ship-breaking yard, across the mounds of

Digging waste oil from pieces of the ship's hull

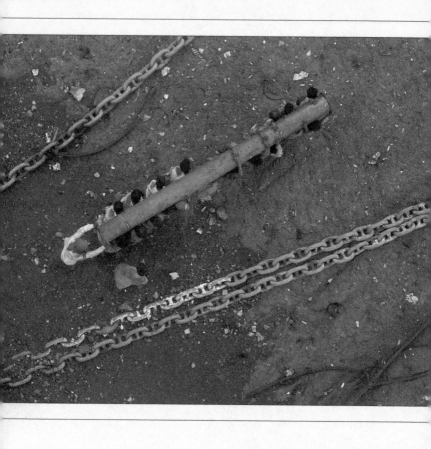

Aerial view of men carrying a pipe

metal, the heads of the workers swaying in unison as they carry steel plates to the bright trucks, to the sea lapping in oil-stained ripples against the shore. Rahman's business card carries a picture of a rich man's gleaming new multimillion-dollar yacht, but he works at the other end of the ship business. He is not a boat builder but the overseer of the destruction of ships. He is the contractor, the middleman between PHP and the foremen like Hakkim. It is Rahman whom the general manager relies on to provide the company with the laborers needed to break up the *Asian Tiger*. He organizes the workforce that toils on the beach in the sun and the rain, all day and all night. There are hundreds of men in the carrying teams, employed through a long chain of middlemen and foremen. By contracts written or sealed only by the word of gentlemen, they are all ultimately tied to Rahman.

The contractor's beard is white, his face smiling and round, and he wears a *punjabi,* the knee-length collarless shirt that in Bangladesh is the mark of the devout Muslim. He goes to pray in the mosque behind the yard five times every day. He has just returned from his lunchtime devotions, and now he stands in his office in front of the blackboard that shows the number of workers on the beach and how much steel they are moving. There are five hundred and fifty-six men working for him that day. In the previous twenty-four hours, just over sixty-seven tons of steel has left the yard.

"Delivery is low at the moment," he says. PHP pays Rahman by the ton moved, so he has a keen interest in the speed of the work. "It's because of the floodwater everywhere: the construction firms don't need much iron."

Heavy rain is holding up building at sites across the country, affecting the whole process of ship breaking, from the work on the beach to the rerolling mills to the ultimate customers, the construction firms building apartments and offices. The irony for the ship breakers is that the best time to run the ships aground is during spring, when the tides are at their highest, but that means the metal is produced during the monsoon. It is a fact of life, and one they can do nothing about.

This year, the floods are bad. Across Bangladesh, the great rivers have burst their banks and spread out across the flat land until fully two-thirds of the districts in the country are under water. This is a double-edged sword for the contractor. There is little demand for the steel the yard is producing—many places where reinforcing rods might be in demand are cut off—but there is a steady stream of men arriving at PHP looking for work.

Tens of millions of people are homeless and hungry. Many are living in crowded makeshift camps set up on the sides of roads built up on embankments. Often that is the only land that remains above water. Hundreds of thousands of acres of paddy fields are useless, the rice crops destroyed. Subsistence farmers, who form a huge proportion of the population, and those who are even worse off, the landless rural laborers, can do little but wait for the rivers to recede. Some try to survive by catching fish washed out of the ponds of fish farms and into the fields and villages. Many flood into the cities, swelling the populations of the slums, begging or pedaling tricycle rickshaws to try to make some cash to buy their next meal. Others come to the ship-breaking yards to keep their families going until the waters recede. For the time being, the foremen's recruitment drives in North Bengal, with their expensive advances and bus trips, can stop. For a while, at least, Rahman has his pick of men.

The *Asian Tiger* is yet to be completely dismantled, but already there is another vessel on the PHP section of the beach north of Chittagong. Mohammed Mohsin, the young owner of the ship-breaking yard, is always scouring the world market for more suitable ships at the right price. He needs vessels that have a flat bottom that will slide easily across the mud when they are run aground so that they will come to rest by the high-water

Cutters on board the Volga

mark. Vessels with sharp keels will stick in the mud and be far too expensive to break up.

The market has been busy this year. Regulations intended to force the owners of the world's fleets to phase out single-hulled tankers are coming into force from the International Maritime Organization and the European Union. The ships are seen as too dangerous, more vulnerable to spills than more modern double-hulled vessels. Many ships that no longer meet the environmental standards of the day have become uneconomical to run and are being sold for scrap.

At the same time, though, prices for ships are rising sharply, which worries all the yard owners. But today, an oil tanker, the *Volga*, is being offered for what still seems reasonable money to Mohsin and he decides to buy her. At 12,500 tons, she is far smaller than the *Asian Tiger*.

Captain Enam is again recruited to pilot the ship as she is brought in. He runs her aground in exactly the correct spot, right next to the remains of the *Asian Tiger*. For a tanker, the *Volga* is a modest size, but she still looms massively on the beach. Her red painted anchor lies on its side in the mud, and the men use the links of the chains as stepping-stones as they skip across the mud to the ladder that leads to the hole that was quickly cut in her side. Once again it is Mohammed Yunnus, the head cutter, who leads the team of men on board. The process of ships dying and being recycled is beginning again.

Piles of steel waiting to be sold

CHAPTER NINE

MOVING ON

All day, every day, trucks drive out through the gates of the PHP ship-breaking yard carrying steel from the *Asian Tiger* on its way to be recycled. They bump up the dirt track to the coast road, splashing through the potholes and shaking the roughly built concrete bungalows and the wood and straw shacks where the night-shift workers try to sleep. There is a sharp right-hand turn by the shop that sells cookies and live chickens that's always tricky for the drivers to negotiate. When it rains hard, the trucks slip and skid in the mud.

A team of office staff at PHP keeps track of the steel as it leaves, making sure the orders are being fulfilled and that no one is pilfering more than has been paid for. Each truck drives over a weigh bridge on its way in and out of the yard, before and after it has been loaded. The difference is written down carefully in a large hard-backed ledger.

The ship-breaking yard isn't computerized, and the work in the PHP office goes on much as it has always been done. The accountants sit in clean, pressed shirts and smart trousers behind shabby desks covered with glass tops, working with pens and paper, filling in the printed books of forms that enable the company to keep track of what is going on. The office is spartan. It has a bare polished concrete floor and whitewashed walls. It's lit by fluorescent lights; they are the locally made ones that cast a greenish light that makes everyone look a bit ill. The only decorations are a PHP calendar and photographs of ships that have been broken earlier at the yard, vessels that are now long gone. The smell of the smoke, oil, and hot metal from the beach drifts in with the breeze off the sea through the open windows. The shouts of the foremen and the distant hum of the men chanting as they work can be heard in the distance. The accountants pause at intervals during the day marked by the snap of the mosque loudspeaker coming on and the sound of the call to prayer singing out. Then they all put on their white woven skullcaps and troop off together to perform their religious obligations.

At lunchtime, their meals are brought from some distant kitchen in tiffin boxes; individual-portion-size stacks of small, round tin plates keep each dish separate and warm. All day, there is a steady stream of more junior employees coming in tentatively for orders from the general manager, who spends most of his time on the phone dealing with the contractors and the customers. When there is no steel leaving the yard, the accountants relax, reading the newspapers, smoking, and drinking hot sweet tea. Gradually, as the weeks turn into months, the amount of steel they record in their ledgers as leaving the yard grows and grows, the total going from thousands of tons to tens of thousands of tons, as what remains of the *Asian Tiger* gets smaller and smaller.

The flat land between the beach and the low, pointy hills is dotted with rerolling mills, where the steel from the ships is melted down into reinforcing rods that will be used to make poured concrete buildings stronger. Bangladesh has been going through several years of major construction. In the big cities of Dhaka and Chittagong, there are building sites on almost every

A fully loaded truck

street corner. A steady supply of steel is vital to keep this development going, and there are few sources other than the ships that arrive on the beach north of Chittagong.

The *Asian Tiger* is rapidly being turned into the raw material for the office blocks and apartments that are mushrooming everywhere. As quickly as it can be cut from the ship, the steel is being processed and put to a new use holding up buildings across the country.

Mohammed Ali is a good customer. Every day, he buys tons and tons of steel from PHP to supply his rerolling mill. The mill is located on the inland side of the coast road, at the same end of the beach as PHP, so transport costs are low. During the day, the metal arrives; truck after truck swings off the road and through the high metal gates into the factory. The trucks are unloaded rapidly and in the same way they were loaded: One man stands on the mound of steel plates with a rod to push; others gather behind the truck with large metal hooks to pull. Straining, they haul the metal out, jumping out of the way as it crashes dangerously to the ground, each lump of steel threatening to trap a foot or a leg. The men are nimble because they have to be. The metal is left in a large untidy pile in the black, gritty factory yard.

Another team of men with blowtorches clambers over the haphazard mound, cutting each piece of steel into more manageable sizes with blowtorches. Slowly and with immense effort, the ship is being broken down further and further, into smaller and smaller pieces. The cutters work from dawn until sunset, until almost the only light left to see by is from the orange sparks that cascade into the puddles the monsoon downpours have formed on the ground.

The men are busy and industrious, but they are only the day shift. Most of the work takes place during the night. Once darkness falls and demand for gas and electricity goes off peak and it becomes cheaper, the ramshackle factories along the coast thunder fully into life.

It is very late, but Mohammed Ali's rerolling mill is working at full speed, filling the night air with glowing light and a rumble. Pairs of men grapple with each piece of steel—now cut into much smaller chunks than when it left the beach, but still painfully heavy—and feed it into an ancient machine that looks rather like a giant pair of mechanical scissors. The machine is linked by long rubber fan belts to a small diesel engine that has been salvaged from some tractor or van. The engine splutters and roars, pumping out smoke from a cracked exhaust. With groans and thuds that shake the ground, the machine's pincers come down again and again, cutting the plates into strips about three feet long by six inches wide—the perfect size to be melted.

The furnace is a huge machine that belches heat and fumes and makes the sweaty, humid night hotter and even stickier. It fills one entire side of the factory, and flames gush from its leaky doors. The glow is orange-hot as the heat escapes toward the corrugated-iron roof of the mill, which is so old it's rusted through in places. Even though the roof has been patched, the rain drips in steadily and sizzles when it lands on hot metal. More blows in on the wind coming through the open sides of the factory. The roof is held up on old metal poles. Men are stationed at the open door of the furnace, getting as close as they can to the flames to thrust in the metal. The heat makes the air furious, and the workers can be seen only indistinctly, shimmering in the haze.

The heat gushing from the open hatch at the far end of the contraption is equally fierce, and that is where Zahid Hasan stands, all night. He is wearing a shirt and a pair of jeans. A large pair of glasses, the kind elderly ladies might wear, and a black-and-white cloth wrapped around his head in a turban provide his only protection from the scorching flames. On his feet he wears no boots, just plastic flip-flop sandals. His job is to reach into the furnace with a long pair of black metal pincers about three feet long and grab a piece of red-hot steel. After being partially melted in the intense heat, it is slightly floppy. Despite the metal's weight, Hasan flicks it out and throws it across the concrete floor to the next man in one smooth movement. For hours on end, he drags out the steel rhythmically, one piece every second or so.

"I've been doing this for twelve years, but we have to be cautious all the time," he shouts above the noise. "Once, in another mill, I saw a piece of steel go right through a man's leg."

The workers think Mohammed Ali's mill is well run, even though there are few concessions to safety by the standards of factories in the developed world.

The man next in the chain grabs the red-hot steel as it slides toward him, and feeds one end of it into a machine. The factory has a series of these rotating rollers mounted side by side in a row. Each is formed of two moving metal wheels, one on top of the other, with a small space in between for the hot steel to pass through. The size of the gaps grows progressively smaller. The metal is fed rapidly, back and forth, back and forth, through each roller and along the row. After each pass, the glowing orange snakes of steel are longer and thinner, slithering out across the factory floor with a clatter. The workers skip to avoid the hot metal, catch the tail ends in their pincers just before they get away, and thrust the rod into the next roller. The molten metal helps to light the whole scene a fiery orange, casting shadows of the men moving and working on the roof of the factory. As the rolling machines roar, giant fans knocked together out of old ship parts provide some cooling breeze. The whole process takes only a few seconds and with the regularity of a clock ticking, a new, finished rod emerges. The last workers in the chain each grab one end of it. They lean back to take the weight and lift it between them before heaving it onto a pile. The steel, now transformed into long rods the thickness of a man's thumb but twenty feet long, slowly cools to a dull gray.

Production goes on at a grueling pace for hours.

"This work is hard," says the furnace man Zahid Hasan, leaning on his pincers during an enforced break. One of the rollers had jammed and the process was brought to a halt while a blowtorch was brought in to free the cooling metal. "But there is no work without hardship."

The owner, Mohammed Ali, is a large man who wears a dirty white shirt and old trousers. He watches carefully as the rods, still slightly warm, are picked up and twisted into bundles by the ragged carrying team.

"The market is sometimes up, sometimes down," he said. "In an up time, we sell six thousand tons in a month. In the rainy season, like now, when construction comes to a halt in many places, we sell six thousand tons in three months."

In the monsoon, the torrential downpours and the flooding across the country make any kind of ship-building work difficult and dangerous. The mill's laborers weigh each bundle on a large set of scales. It is the old-fashioned mechanical type with a big round face and a needle. Mohammed Ali says his profit is one hundred taka ($1.60) a ton. Even in the low season, he is doing well.

During the night, the trucks that had brought the steel plates from the yard return to take away the finished product. When everyone pulls in through the gates, the carriers leap into action to load it. The men stand in a line down its side and, bundle by bundle, pick up the heavy rods on their right, lift them over their heads, and throw them into the back. A worker scampers about on top of the load, tugging and pulling the bundles, rearranging the steel, balancing as each new bundle's landing makes the vehicle shake on its axles. Each truck is full within just twenty minutes or so. Its engine erupts into life, and the driver maneuvers carefully back out onto the coast road. The steel had been in the rerolling mill for just hours. A few days ago, it was still part of the *Asian Tiger*. Now it is headed out again, pieces of the oil tanker being scattered across towns and cities all over Bangladesh. Tomorrow, it could be supporting a new building.

Mohammed Ali, the rerolling mill owner, smiles. "It's a matter of happiness to me that all the rods are from our own mills. I want new buildings built in the country," he says. "It's definitely a good thing, because if we don't use these old ships, they'll turn into dust."

The steel rods from the ships are used on construction sites across the big cities. Low-rise six- or seven-story apartment blocks are going up everywhere, in the capital and Chittagong and towns like Syhet, in the northeast. It is a building boom, unplanned, unregulated, and at least partially fueled by money earned on the black market. Bangladesh is one of the most corrupt countries on earth. Bribes and kickbacks have to be laundered and hidden somewhere.

The new buildings are all being made of reinforced concrete. Along the roadsides of towns and suburbs, the rods made from the *Asian Tiger* and other ships are untangled and laid out in straight lines. All day, small boys and apprentices squat down to hammer them straight again. Alongside them, teams of women work, squatting on piles of bricks, hammering them into chips to be used as aggregate in concrete. Buying stones in Bangladesh is more expensive than employing scores of people to make brick chips by hand. There is almost nowhere that the residents of the cities can go to escape the endless clanging and the chinking, or the dust and grime that hang in the air, but that is the price of progress.

To make each pillar, the builders first put the rods in place. They are twisted and tied together into the rough shape laid out in the plans. The rods will be the bones of the building, giving the structure strength. Then carpenters make a boxlike wooden frame around the rods, which will be used as a mold. Finally, men wearing loincloths carry up the concrete from the street below, where it was mixed. They form chains, each man walking up one ladder before passing his load of concrete to the next. They carry it on their heads in wide, flat, iron dishes. The worker at the top receives each dish as it arrives and tips its contents into place. Gradually, the wooden mold is filled, and in this way the buildings grow toward the sky at a surprisingly rapid pace. But it is excruciatingly hard work in the hot sun and it can be dangerous, too. There are as few safety standards on Bangladeshi building sites as there are in the ship-breaking yards.

The floors of the buildings are put together in a similar way. First, the wooden boxes for the concrete are hammered together. They are held in place by a forest of bamboo that is wedged vertically between the existing floor and the new one. The poles are placed just a foot or so apart to hold the weight. Then the steel rods are laid in a grid pattern inside the molds. Finally, the concrete that will form the floor is poured on top. After it hardens, the bamboo will be taken away. It is a quick method of building, and above all, it's cheap.

So many of these apartment blocks are springing up that some parts of the cities look like war zones. They are filled with jagged half-made buildings and empty window frames. But the men who work in the ship-breaking yard and the rerolling mill and on the construction sites will not be able to afford to live in them. A new Bangladesh is being built on the back of their labor. They still live in huts made of straw and corrugated iron.

The *Asian Tiger* is not just a source of the steel badly needed by Bangladesh's economy; there are other useful metals in the

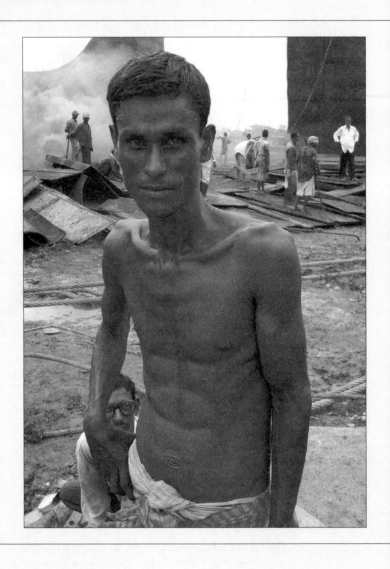

Propeller cutter Mohammed Motin

hulk that had once been a great ship. One of the most valuable parts is the propeller, and the *Asian Tiger*'s weighed forty tons or more. It was dragged up the beach through the mud by winch. The job was difficult because the edges of the wings kept digging in, but eventually the ship breakers got it above the high-water mark and it lay there, huge and immobile like a giant's toy that had been cast away. Children played on it sometimes, climbing up and down. The metal was a dull golden color, and there were small scars on the leading edges, where the propeller had snagged on objects out in the great oceans or in the ports of the world. Propellers are specially designed for each individual ship, so they can't just be sold and bolted onto another vessel. They have to be cut up.

One day, a three-man team comes to the beach carrying sledgehammers and an old cloth tool bag full of chisels. These men are specialists in breaking up propellers without damaging the bronze alloy. They move from yard to yard, up and down the coast, working to contract. Two of the three, Mohammed Motin and Mohammed Mohsin (who is no relation to PHP's owner) have been sculpted by their hard work. They don't carry an ounce of fat on their bodies, and the fibers of each of their muscles seem to stand out on their slender frames. Even their faces are spare and lean.

"It's not possible to cut the propeller by gas," says Mohammed Motin, as both men lean on their heavy sledgehammers before beginning their work. "This is very valuable material, and if we use flames, we may lose quality, so we do it by hand."

The third member of the team, Mohammed Korshed Alam, has the physically easier but riskier job. He carefully places one of the chisels between the jaws of a set of long iron pincers and looks up when he is ready. His friends begin to work. Standing side by side on the propeller, they raise their sledgehammers above their heads and bring them down one after another in rapid succession. *Clang, clang, clang.* Every time, the heavy metal hammerheads skim past Mohammed Korshed Alam's unprotected skull as he crouches at their feet, moving his chisel an inch farther along between each blow.

"I'm not worried, because we are experienced," he shouts above the noise. "I trust them, and we've never had any accidents."

They are making imperceptible dents in the bronze with each blow, but gradually a slot is forming across the blade. In places, the metal is ten inches thick, and it seems an impossibly long job for the three men to undertake.

"It'll take us from eight o'clock this morning until tomorrow lunchtime to finish this one cut," says Mohammed Motin. "We have to break this blade of the propeller into twenty-six pieces, and there are three more blades to go."

The market for old propellers is global. W. K. Chung has traveled to the beach from South Korea on a mission to buy up the alloy.

"My business is in nonferrous metals," he says. "I'd like to buy material; I always want to buy something."

Chung's visits to Bangladesh are so frequent that he has bought a house in Chittagong.

"The price may go down, or it may go up," Chung says. "But we always need raw material or the factories can't make new products."

Mohammed Mohsin has come to meet Chung, and they disappear into an office for private negotiations about the price. They emerge shortly afterward, shaking hands.

"Take a sample of the alloy," says Mohammed Mohsin. "Test it to check it's as good quality as we think it is."

Once the men breaking up the propeller finish their work, the pieces will be loaded into containers and shipped to a factory,

The propeller-cutting team

perhaps in South Korea, perhaps in some other part of the world. The alloy will be melted down in a special furnace, so as not to alter its consistency, and recast into new propellers to be fitted to new ships. Then the bronze will resume its journey around the seas, churning the water into a wake again, after a short break on the beach north of Chittagong.

The remains of the Asian Tiger *from the stern*

CHAPTER TEN

LAST DAYS

For the workers on the beach it is a day much like any other. For the *Asian Tiger*, it is her last. For weeks, just the few broken remnants of what had been the stern of the ship remained, lying in a tangle of metal far out on the mudflats. Progress had slowed almost to nothing as the cutters did the complicated work of dismantling the engine room with all its pipes and walkways. The smaller parts of the great machine had been unbolted and unscrewed, the old stubborn fixings coaxed apart. They were carried off to be sold whole and used as spares. The massive iron engine block had presented a major challenge with the risk of fire from the traces of the oil that had lubricated the workings as the ship plowed across the oceans. But it had been hauled up to the beach and cut into rectangular metal sheets like all the rest of the ship before it.

The first piece of the *Asian Tiger* to be removed had been a large section of the side of her hull; the last was the joint where the massive propeller had been attached to the great iron shaft that led to the engine. One day, shortly before the Muslim festival of Eid ul-Fitr, it was dragged off the mudflats on the end of a long steel cable attached to the one of the winches. The *Asian Tiger* had died long ago; the life had left her when her engines went quiet soon after she was rammed onto the beach. Now her corpse had been disposed of.

There is little ceremony to mark the passing of the great ship. No goats are sacrificed, no children gather on the beach to watch the event and eat the sweets handed out by the owner as is customary when a new ship arrives. Few of the men even turn around from their work to look. There is still much to keep them busy. The *Volga*, the tanker that arrived in the yard a couple of months after the *Asian Tiger*, is nearing completion, too. The second ship's hull is still being broken, and large pieces of steel are being dragged up to the beach. The cutters there are busy slicing it into smaller sections, and the carrying teams have plenty of work to do to keep up, moving the steel around the yard.

Mohammed Yunnus, the chief cutter, is supervising the operation. From first thing in the morning, he clambers all over the ship. The way up to the deck is via a precarious exposed metal ladder and through a hatch onto the deck. Yunnus regularly pops his head through to check on progress and to chivvy on his men. At times he can be found holding his own blowtorch against the steel, doing some of the work himself. These days he is wearing a hard hat salvaged from some ship's locker with the word "Captain" written in felt-tip pen across the front of it.

"It was a good feeling to have finished the great ship," he says, looking at the space where the *Asian Tiger* had been. Then he shrugs. In truth, it has been nothing particularly special to him.

During his years on the beach, Yunnus has seen more than eighty ships arrive at full speed with their propellers thumping the water to drive them on, and leave again in pieces on the shoulders of the men. Some of them were bigger than the *Asian Tiger*. More important to Yunnus is the fact that his sons are still in school and their education is still on track. His family is still moving forward. Now that the eldest has completed Class Six,

Last days of the Asian Tiger

Yunnus is a step closer to realizing his dream of seeing them start their adult lives with better opportunities than he had been given. Yunnus is still waiting to build his brick house, but he has hope he will achieve that ambition, too. As long as there are ships in the yard, there will be work for skilled men like him.

It is the Islamic holy month of Ramadan, and all the workers, including Yunnus, are fasting. From dawn until dusk, they neither eat nor drink, not even sips of water. Chittagong is well within the tropics, and it is hot on the beach, despite the fact that it is the beginning of what passes for winter in Bangladesh. The sun shines down in a white glare all day, the blue sky unbroken by clouds. The cooler months are also the dry season.

The men are constantly hungry and thirsty. Every evening, they gather to break their fast, with sticky sweet dates and the traditional fried snacks of eggplant and chickpea salad. The meal is known as Iftaar, and they all keenly look forward to it during their shifts. Today, as they leave their places of work on the ship and on the beach, their smiles are broader than those usually worn by men looking forward to their first meal for hours. As the shifts end, each worker is handed a bonus of five hundred taka ($8) to mark the end of the *Asian Tiger*. It is as much as most make in a week.

Almost all the men are working on the beach in order to support wives and families back home in the countryside of North Bengal. This month, they will be able to send a little bit extra. But they also keep some of the money, for which they have worked so hard, to treat themselves.

Later in the evening, some congregate in the village behind the ship-breaking yard to eat together. Almost every small group of roommates has bought some special food to celebrate. They have been out to get chickens, which now lie limp on the floor, still whole and with their feathers on. Poultry is always slaughtered in front of the shopper in Bangladesh, and the birds are still warm, the carcasses bloodied from when their throats were slashed with small sharp knives. Some men have even bought a little beef, a real treat after the plain rice and lentils they eat most other days. The meals are cooked in steaming pots and eaten by the hungry workers with their fingers. The workers don't talk much. They just shovel in the food as quickly as possible.

A popular way to spend the bonus is to head off to the brothels in Chittagong. The men board ramshackle buses in boisterous groups for the journey into the city. Their destination is the downmarket establishments in the poorest districts of the town. The brothels they can afford are in the slums, down muddy alleyways, through a maze of ramshackle tin huts. The areas are gloomy, with each dwelling lit by a single bare low-watt bulb. It is hard to distinguish the brothels from people's homes but the men know the way well and walk on until they arrive at a larger tin building. It is still just a shack, with a series of doors leading off from a filthy, unpaved courtyard. Each door is the way into a girl's room.

The prostitutes are standing around, trying to look alluring to attract customers. Some of the boldest are wearing Western-style jeans and T-shirts, a rare sight in Bangladesh, where women wear either saris or baggy, all-covering trousers and long blouses. The outfit is called a *shalwar kameez*. The prices for a prostitute start at fifty taka (80 cents), but five hundred ($8) can buy one of the most desirable girls. Pale skin and plumpness are valued highly by the men, who have been scorched dark by the sun and left skinny through hard labor and limited food.

When the men return to the beach late at night, telling ribald tales and blue jokes, the work is still going on out on the dark beach. The landscape is lit only by the hot blue light of the blowtorches and the orange sparks as men continue to cut up larger chunks of metal. The outlines of the steel pile up haphazardly, and the men moving around cast dark shadows on the sides of the ships. Not a trace of the *Asian Tiger* that is recognizable remains. The expanse of mud she occupied is completely empty but for streaks of oil.

It has taken less than six months to tear the ship apart. When she arrived, she had seemed indestructible, a huge solid vessel that dwarfed the men who worked on her, making them look and feel as insignificant as ants. But they had made short work of her; it was extraordinary what could be done in a very short time simply by bringing together enough men. Much of the metal that had made up the ship was put to other uses long ago. The more valuable alloys, such as those found in the propeller, had been broken up and exported. It was being forged anew for another ship. Most of the steel had been driven away in the back of trucks and melted down, scattered to towns and cities across Bangladesh. But a significant proportion of the metal that had formed the *Asian Tiger* remains in the ship-breaking yard.

The dry sand and dust at the top of the beach, above the high water mark, is now covered with steel plates. Each plate is the size of a billiard table and about an inch thick. The plates are laid on top of each other in piles around five feet tall. Pathways have been left between them for the men to walk down and to give the trucks access for loading. The market for steel in Bangladesh is slow, and seven thousand tons of the ship remain to be sold. It is a change that threatens the livelihoods of everyone working in the ship-breaking yards.

For Mojibur Rahman, the contractor, the downturn in demand for the steel that is being produced on the beach is a serious problem. The market has not picked up as he had hoped it would after the normal lull during the annual monsoon. He is paid by PHP by the weight of steel that leaves the yard, and his operation runs in its most efficient manner when the men can simply pick up the plates from where they are cut and load them straight onto a waiting truck. Storage means each piece of steel has to be carried twice before it leaves the beach, once to the piles where it will be kept and a second time to the truck for delivery when a buyer is eventually found. Repeated time and time again, it is a significant increase in his costs.

Mojibur Rahman's large face wears a worried expression; his forehead is puckered by anxiety. His company has taken a small advance from PHP to tide him over, but it will not last for long.

"I'm losing money, but I'm carrying on in order to maintain my position here," he says as he pores over the figures in his ledger, all of them bad. "If this goes on, the future may not be happy for me."

Mojibur Rahman has five hundred and ninety-six men on the beach today. He has to pay them all, and he will not make a profit. In the good times, years ago, he says he employed more than a thousand and still had plenty of money left over for himself.

Market forces sweeping around the world are rippling onto the beach north of Chittagong. There is a worldwide shortage of steel because of the huge economic growth of China, a country searching all corners of the earth for resources to devour. Construction needs metal, and lots of it, and demand is huge. It is the middle of a kind of global gold rush, but this time the resource being sought after so eagerly is steel. So high is the demand for the product, which is made by smelting iron ore if it is not acquired by recycling, that twenty percent of the global supply is being used to build new steel mills. One of China's sources of the metal is the old scrap ships that the breaking yards on the Chittagong beach rely on, too.

Once, decades earlier, when the breaking yards had started up in Chittagong, the ships had been almost given away. Now the competition to buy each one coming onto the market is fierce. The men who run the yards, like Mohammed Mohsin, are still managing to pick up a few, but at a higher price, and they have to pass on their increased costs to their customers. For now, the steel

Pieces of the Asian Tiger *laid out on the beach*

rods they produce are simply too expensive for the local market. They have gone up in price threefold in a year. Bangladeshi building firms, who use the bulk of the metal, face real difficulties. They tend to work to a fixed cost. They had quoted a price to complete an entire building when the cost of reinforcing rods was lower. Now the price of steel, one of their major raw components, is so high, many are unable to make a profit. Their only solution is to stop work and wait. Many have laid off their workers while they sit out the hard times, hoping prices will fall again. The pace of building in Bangladesh's towns and cities has slowed, the skylines no longer echoing day and night with the clanging of hammers and the thump as foundation piles are driven into the ground. So the ship breakers are chasing a reduced supply of ships at a higher cost, and they are selling their steel to fewer customers. China's rush for growth is slowing the pace of development of the economies of other countries that can't keep up, including Bangladesh.

The effects of that distant upheaval are being felt as far away as the poorest districts of Bangladesh, in North Bengal, where for years men have looked to the ship-breaking yards as an escape from poverty and hunger. Little seems to have changed in the villages over the centuries. People still till the fields by hand and fish in the ponds with nets, living hand to mouth. Few there, apart from those who go to Chittagong, think much about the world beyond the next hamlet, but even they are not immune to China's dominance.

Hakkim, the foreman, has gone back to his home village just before Eid, traveling the hundreds of kilometers by bus again, until he finally arrives in the place where he grew up. This year, Ramadan coincides with the season known in the countryside as the Monga—the Hunger—and many men are waiting for his arrival. The agricultural calendar of planting and harvesting leaves a gap at a certain time of the year. Most people in North Bengal are day laborers in the fields, and they are employed only when jobs need to be done. With no work available, they are getting desperate, and their bellies have grown pinched with famine. Some migrate to the towns to pull rickshaws or beg. Others hope for work on the beach breaking up the ships. But Hakkim has come for only a handful of men this time. On earlier trips he had recruited around seventy. After speaking to Hakkim, many return to their tin shacks, disappointed to wait out the weeks until the cycle of sowing and reaping resumes and the fields make them busy again.

The men who get rich from ship breaking are starting to get a little concerned, too. One evening, as the *Asian Tiger* is being finished off, a group of yard owners, including Mohammed Mohsin, gather in a restaurant in Chittagong—Bonanza. Bonanza was built in better times by several of their number, the name inspired by the boom period they were enjoying then. The city had few decent restaurants, so the yard owners had decided to set up their own. It was also somewhere to meet, something to give them an excuse to get together. It was a fun little project dreamed up by men flush with money.

Despite the downturn, none of them is doing too badly. They wear fancy Rolex or Cartier watches and sharply cut suits, and have the look of prosperous men, with their thick hair and shiny cheeks. They have all diversified their businesses over the years, and so none of them is entirely reliant on ship breaking. But the work on the beach is still the backbone of their conglomerates, and they can see that a slowdown in the supply of steel will have an impact all through the economy. Even rich men like them could be touched by it.

Already in the construction industry the owners' association is going to strike to protest the high cost of raw materials. It is a futile gesture, a hangover from resistance to colonialism that had worked to persuade the British to leave. But the global economy is impervious to their protests. The ship-breaking owners have another idea. They want the government to reduce the cost of the gas they use to fire their blowtorches in the yards. It is five hundred taka ($8) per canister, a major part of their costs. There are huge fields of natural gas under the sea out in the Bay of Bengal, they reason. Why not use this gas to kick-start their industry and, through it, the entire economy? But Bangladesh's government is impoverished, and there is little it can do to help, even if it wanted to. The businessmen will have to get through the bad times on their own.

Mohsin sits in his small cubbyhole of an office, next door to his father's not much bigger room in the PHP building in old Chittagong. He is looking at a page of figures printed off by the accountants and tapping at the calculator on his desk. He is working out the sums, finding out if he has made or lost money from the vast operation to break up the *Asian Tiger*. It is not looking like good news so far. After all the effort of buying the ship and the work of the men on the beach, he is running a loss of around $200,000. Once the steel from the ship being stored on the beach has been sold he will break even or perhaps, if he is lucky, make a small profit. But Mohsin says the numbers do not matter to PHP too much. They can subsidize the operation for years from the other businesses in the company. The float-glass factory is nearing completion, the oxygen plant is doing well, and there is the shipping line that he is busy setting up.

For Mohsin, the key factor with ship breaking—the reason he and the other entrepreneurs stay in it at all—is the cash flow it generates for a company. No one in the industry ever asks for credit, and all the metal is bought for cold, hard cash. Sometimes Mohsin receives $800,000 in a single day. Keeping the money coming in is vital in a country where expensive bank loans and an almost inoperative stock exchange make the lack of capital a major obstacle to business. Mohsin has already bought five more ships to keep the yard busy and the cash flowing. These ships are much smaller than the *Asian Tiger*, though, around a third of her size, reflecting the more difficult times. And he has paid far more than he would have had to a year earlier.

PHP is now considering getting out of ship-breaking one day, of leaving the business that started it all. The chairman, Mizanur Rahman, who laid the foundations of his fortune on the beach, has his eyes turned firmly toward the future. The company and the country are developing, he believes, to the point where the brutal, messy work of recycling the ships could end; when Bangladesh can get the resources it needs without damaging its environment and risking the health and lives of its people so much; when the source of the nation's steel will not be old ships but iron-bearing rock imported from abroad for processing.

"We are building an iron ore plant," he says. "It will require an investment of a billion dollars, but then this ship-breaking business can stop."

The men working the beach are unaware of the calculations of their masters. They are happy simply to have all survived another year. And as they carouse that night, their bellies full of food, some just back from spending their small bonuses in the brothels, they tell each other how lucky they have been because there have been no serious accidents on the *Asian Tiger*. A few weeks before, a group of cutters in one of the yards down the beach owned by another company were killed in an explosion that had suddenly torn through the fuel tank of a ship. Nothing like that has happened on PHP's stretch of the beach. One man had broken his leg when a gas bottle fell on him, but that was it. The *Asian Tiger* had not wanted vengeance for her death on the beach. She had not demanded blood.

INDEX

The author with workers in the shipyards

Roland Buerk is a BBC correspondent in South Asia, based in Bangladesh. He has also reported from Afghanistan and Sri Lanka. On the twenty-sixth of December, 2004, he was in Unawatuna, in Sri Lanka, and narrowly survived the tsunami, which left three hundred people dead in that village alone. His writing has appeared in *The Times* of London, *The Economist,* and the *Financial Times*. This is his first book.